PUBLICATIONS OF THE UNIVERSITY OF MANCHESTER

HISTORICAL SERIES

No. VII.

Studies and Notes supplementary to Stubbs' Constitutional History

SHERRATT & HUGHES
Publishers to the Victoria University of Manchester
Manchester: 34 Cross Street
London: 60 Chandos Street, W.C.

Studies and Notes supplementary to Stubbs' Constitutional History

Down to the Great Charter

BY

CHARLES PETIT-DUTAILLIS

Honorary Professor in the University of Lille
Rector of the University of Grenoble

TRANSLATED BY

W. E. RHODES M.A.

Formerly Jones Fellow in History

MANCHESTER
AT THE UNIVERSITY PRESS
1908

UNIVERSITY OF MANCHESTER PUBLICATIONS
No. XXXVIII.

PREFACE TO THE ENGLISH TRANSLATION.

THE twelve studies and notes here printed have been translated from the French of Professor Ch. Petit-Dutaillis in order to provide the English student with a supplement to the first volume of Bishop Stubbs' "Constitutional History of England."

The recent appearance of the first volume of a French translation of that classical work, almost exactly a quarter of a century after the publication of the corresponding volume of the original, is good evidence that it still remains the standard treatise on its subject. At the same time, the fact that M. Petit-Dutaillis, the editor of the French edition, has found it necessary to append over 130 closely printed pages by way of addition and correction shows that the early part of the book, at all events, has not escaped the ravages of time. The twenty-five years which have elapsed since it appeared have seen much fruitful research both in England and abroad upon the period which it covers. Continental scholars such as Fustel de Coulanges and Meitzen and in this country Maitland, Seebohm, Round, Vinogradoff, and others have added greatly to our knowledge of the origin and early history of English institutions. The results of this research so far as it had proceeded in Stubbs' lifetime were very imperfectly incorporated by him in the successive editions of his book. Moreover, as M. Petit-Dutaillis points out in his preface, the study of these institutions is now approached from a standpoint different from that which was taken by Stubbs and his contemporaries. Some portions of the first volume of the "Constitutional

History " have, therefore, become obsolete and others require correction and readjustment.

Teachers and students of English constitutional history have long been embarrassed by a text-book which, while indispensable as a whole, is in many points out of date. Hitherto they have had to go for newer light to a great variety of books and periodicals. English historians were apparently too much engrossed with detailed research to stop and sum up the advances that had been made. It has been left to a French scholar to supply the much-needed survey. M. Petit-Dutaillis, who was, at the time when he brought out the first volume of his edition, Professor of History in the University of Lille, but has quite recently been appointed Rector of the University of Grenoble, had already shown an intimate and scholarly acquaintance with certain periods of English history in his " Etude sur la vie et le règne de Louis VIII." and in his elaborate introduction to the work of his friend André Réville on the Peasants' Revolt of 1381. The twelve "additional studies and notes " in which he brings the first volume of the "Constitutional History" abreast of more recent research meet so obvious a need and, in their French dress, have been so warmly welcomed by English scholars, that it has been thought desirable to make them easily accessible to the many students of history who may not wish to purchase the rather expensive volume of the French edition in which they are included.

M. Petit-Dutaillis willingly acceded to the suggestion and has read the proofs of the translation. The extracts from his preface, given elsewhere, explain more fully than has been done above the reasons for and the nature of the revision of Stubbs' work which he has carried out.

As M. Petit-Dutaillis observes, in speaking of the French version of the " Constitutional History," the translation of books of this kind can only be competently executed by historians. It has in this case been entrusted to a graduate of the University of Manchester, Mr. W. E. Rhodes, who has himself done good historical work. I have carefully revised it, corrected, with the author's approval, one or two small slips in the French text, substituted for its references to the French translation of the "Constitutional History" direct references to the last edition (1903) of the first volume of the original, and added in square brackets a few references to Professor Vinogradoff's "English Society in the Eleventh Century," which appeared after the publication of the French edition. The index has been adapted by Mr. Rhodes from the one made by M. Lefebvre for that edition.

JAMES TAIT.

THE UNIVERSITY,
    MANCHESTER,
        September 8th, 1908.

EXTRACTS FROM THE AUTHOR'S PREFACE.

THE French edition of the " Constitutional History " of William Stubbs is intended for the use of the students of our Faculties of Arts and Law . . . The "Constitutional History" is a classic and the readers of the "Bibliothèque internationale de Droit public"[1] have seen it more than once quoted as a book the authority of which is accepted without discussion. It seems desirable, however, to emphasize the exceptional merits of this great work as well as to draw attention to its weak points and, as it is not an adaptation but a translation— complete and reverent—that is given here, to explain why we have thought some additions indispensable . . . All that we know of Stubbs inspires confidence, confidence in the solidity and extent of his knowledge, the honesty of his criticism, the sureness of his judgment, the depth of his practical experience of men and things. Despite the merit of his other works, and especially of the prefaces which he wrote for the *Chronicles* he edited, Stubbs only showed the full measure of his powers in the " Constitutional History." It is the fruit of prodigious labour, of a thorough investigation of all the printed sources which a historian could consult at the period when these three bulky volumes successively appeared. It is an admirable storehouse of facts, well chosen, and set forth with scrupulous good faith. The word " Constitution " is taken in its widest sense. How the England of the Renascence with its strong Monarchy, its House of Lords, its local institutions, its Church, its Nobility, its towns, its freeholders and its villeins was evolved from the old Anglo-Saxon Britain,

1. In which the translation is included.

this is the subject of the author's enquiry. With the exception of diplomatic and military history he touches upon the most diverse subjects. His book is at once a scientific manual of institutions and, at least from the Norman Conquest onwards, a continuous history of every reign. Mr. Maitland has called attention to the advantages of the plan which by combining narrative and analysis allows no detail of importance to escape, and gives a marvellously concrete impression of the development of the nation.[2]

Does this imply that the perusal of the "Constitutional History" leaves us nothing to desire? The French who have kept the " classical " spirit and reserve their full admiration for that which is perfectly clear, will doubtless find that his thought is very often obscure and his conclusions undecided. This is really one result of the vast erudition and the good faith of the author. This honest historian is so careful not to neglect any document, so impressed with the complexity of the phenomena that he does not always succeed in disposing them in an absolutely coherent synthesis . . . .

But inconsistencies of view and the relative obscurity of certain passages are not the only fault which impairs Stubbs' work. There is another, at once more serious and more easily remedied, a fault which is particularly felt in the first volume. The book is no longer up to date. The chapters dealing with the Anglo-Saxon period, especially, have become obsolete on many points. The revisions effected by Stubbs in the successive editions which he published down to his death, are insufficient. They do not always give an accurate idea of the progress made by research, and they are not even executed with all the attention to details which is desirable. Although the author had not ceased to be interested in history the task of revision obviously repelled him. The "Constitutional History" has grown

2, Maitland, *Eng. Hist. Rev.*, xvi., 1901, p. 422.

out of date in yet another way. Stubbs wrote history on lines on which it is no longer written by the great mediævalists of to-day. He belonged to the liberal generation which had seen and assisted in the attainment of electoral reforms in England and of revolutionary and nationalist movements on the Continent. He had formed himself, in his youth, under the discipline of the patriotic German scholars who saw in the primitive German institutions the source of all human dignity and of all political independence. He thought he saw in the development of the English Constitution the magnificent and unique expansion of these first germs of self-government, and England was for him "the messenger of liberty to the world." The degree to which this optimistic and patriotic conception of English history could falsify, despite the author's scrupulous conscientiousness, his interpretation of the sources, is manifest in the pages which he devoted to the Great Charter. Nowadays when so many illusions have been dissipated, when parliamentary institutions, set up by almost every civilized nation, have more openly revealed, as they developed, their inevitable littlenesses and when the formation of nationalities has turned Europe into a camp, history is written with less enthusiasm. The motives of the deeds accomplished by our forefathers are scrutinized with cold impartiality, minute care is taken to grasp the precise significance which they had at the time when they were done, and lastly the economic conception of history exercises a certain influence even over those who do not admit its principles. Open the " History of English Law " of Sir Frederick Pollock and Mr. Maitland, the masterpiece of contemporary English learning, written twenty years after the " Constitutional History " and note the difference of tone.

This French edition being intended for the use of students and persons little versed in mediæval history, it was necessary to let them know that the work is not

PREFACE

always abreast of the progress of research and we have thought it possible to furnish them, although in a very modest measure, with the means of acquiring supplementary information . . . [3]

I have specially written for this publication a dozen studies and additional notes. Some of these lay claim to no originality, and their only purpose is to summarize celebrated controversies or to call attention to recent discoveries. In others a study of English history of some duration has allowed me to express a personal opinion on certain questions. The problems most discussed by the scholars who are now investigating the Anglo-Saxon, Norman, and Angevin periods have thus been restated with a bibliography which may be useful . . .

M. Bémont, the Frenchman who has the best knowledge of mediæval England, has been good enough to read the proofs of the additional studies.

CH. PETIT-DUTAILLIS.

3. M. Petit-Dutaillis proceeds to state that he has added to Stubbs' notes references to works and editions by French scholars "which he was unacquainted with, or at least treated as non-existent," and has referred the reader to better editions of English Chronicles and other sources where Stubbs was content to use inferior ones, or where critical editions have appeared since his death.

CONTENTS.

I.

THE EVOLUTION OF THE RURAL CLASSES IN ENGLAND AND THE ORIGIN OF THE MANOR.

AT the end of the Middle Ages, rural England was divided into estates, which were known by the Norman

The manor at the end of the Middle Ages. name of *manors*.[1] The manor, a purely private division,[2] a unit in the eyes of its lord, did not necessarily coincide with the township or village, a legal division of the hundred and a unit in the eyes of the king; but, except in certain counties,[3] the two areas were normally identical. In each of his manors, the lord of the manor retained some lands in demesne, which he cultivated with the aid of labour services, and he let the remainder in return for fixed dues, to the tenants, free or villein, who formed the village community.[4] Agriculture and cattle-rearing

1. The term is not absolutely general. At the end of the 12th century it is not used in the Boldon Book, the land-book of the Bishop of Durham; the rural unit, in this document, is the *villa*, though in reality the manorial organisation existed. (Lapsley, in *Victoria History of the Counties of England, Durham*, i, 1905, pp. 262, 268.)

2. Maitland, *Select Pleas in Manorial Courts*, 1889, i, p. xxxix.

3. In the counties of Cambridge, Essex, Suffolk, Norfolk, Lincoln, Nottingham and Derby, and in some parts of Yorkshire, the village was frequently divided between three or four Norman lords, at least at the date of *Domesday Book* (Maitland, *Domesday Book and Beyond*, 1897, pp. 22–23). The co-existence of several manors in the territory of one village sometimes brought about the partition of the village; or on the other hand it persisted, and was the cause of frequent disputes; see on this subject Vinogradoff, *The Growth of the Manor*, 1905, pp. 304 sqq.; *Villainage in England*, 1892, pp. 393 sqq.; Maitland, *Domesday Book and Beyond*, pp. 129 sqq.

4. See the description of the manorial organisation in Vinogradoff, *Growth of the Manor*, pp. 307 sqq., and *Villainage*, pp. 223 sqq. [Cf. also his *English Society in the Eleventh Century*, 1908, pp. 353 sqq.] Mr. Maitland has published an excellent monograph on the Manor of Wilburton in the *English Historical Review*, 1894, pp. 417 sqq. Numerous monographs of this kind would be very useful.

A

were carried on according to the system of the un-enclosed field, the open field.[1] In the manor there were several fields alternatively left fallow or sown with different crops.[2] Each of these fields, instead of belonging as a whole to a single tenant, was divided, by means of balks of turf, into narrow strips of land, whose length represented the traditional length of furrow made by the plough before it was turned round. The normal holding of a peasant was made up of strips of arable land scattered in the different fields, customary rights in the common lands, and a part of the fodder produced by the meadows of the village. Once the harvest had been reaped in the fields and the hay got in in the meadows, the beasts were sent there for common pasture. Every one had to conform to the same rules, to the same method of rotation of crops; even the lord of the manor, who often had a part of his private demesne situated in the open field.

The Open Field.

Whatever progress individualism had made in the 13th century, the inhabitant of a village was a member of a community whose rights and interests restricted his own, and which, in its relation to the lord of the manor, still remained powerful.[3] Common business was discussed periodically in the *hall* of the manor, and the villeins, the English term for the serfs, attended the *halimot* just as much as the free tenants; although the villeins were in a majority, the free tenants were amenable to this court in which we see the peasants themselves " presenting " the members of

The Village Community.

1. The English open-field system has been often studied. The starting point is Nasse's essay *Zur Geschichte der mittelalterlichen Feldgemein-schaft in England*, 1869. F. Seebohm revived the subject in his celebrated book, to which we shall have to refer again : *The English Village Community*, 1883, pp. 1 sqq. See *ibid.*, pp. 2 and 4, the map and sketch made from nature—for there still exist some relics of these methods of cultivation. Cf. Mr. Vinogradoff's chapter on the Open-field System, in *The Growth of the Manor*, pp. 165 sqq. ; Stubbs, i, pp. 52 sqq., 89 sqq.

2. For example : corn—barley or oats,—fallow.

3. See Vinogradoff, *Growth of the Manor*, pp. 318 sqq., 361 sqq. and passim ; *Villainage*, pp. 354 sqq.

the community who had done their work ill. The reason is that the community as a whole was answerable to its lord. Sometimes, moreover, the village, like the free towns, farmed the dues and paid a fixed lump sum to its lord. It was, then, a juridical person.[1] Finally, the village had its share in local government, police and the royal courts of justice.[2]

Thus the English manor, like a French rural domain of the same period, was dependent on a lord; and the lord claimed dues from his tenants and day-work to till the land which he cultivated himself. But the customs to which the exercise of the right of ownership had to defer, the methods of husbandry and pasturage, the importance of the interests of all kinds entrusted to the peasants themselves, showed the singular strength of the English rural community.

What was the origin of this manorial organization, of the usages of the open field, of the condition of the freemen and villeins, of this village community which had the rights of a juridical person and formed the primordial unit of local government?

The question of the origin of the seignorial and manorial system, which, in the history of the whole of the West, is a subject of controversy, is *Obscurity of the question of origins.* particularly obscure and complex in England, because England underwent only a partial Romanisation which is imperfectly known, and the exact extent and character of which it is impossible to estimate.

The " Romanists " and " Germanists " of the other side of the Channel engage in battles in which analogy and hypothesis are the principal weapons; and the projectiles are not mortal to either of the two armies.

The Germanists deny any importance in the develop-

1. We adopt on this point the views of Mr. Vinogradoff, *Growth of the Manor*, pp. 322 sqq.

2. Stubbs, *Const. Hist.*, i. pp. 88 sqq., 102, 115, 128, etc.

ment of English institutions to the Roman element, as

The Germanist thesis. The Mark. indeed also to the Celtic. The earliest of them sought to explain the formation of the rural community and even that of the manor by the Mark theory.[1] Several years before the appearance of the famous works of G. L. von Maurer on the *Mark-verfassung in Deutschland,* Kemble in his *Saxons in England,* drew a picture, somewhat vague in outline it is true, of a Saxon England divided into *marks,* inhabited by communities of free Saxons, associated of their own free will for the cultivation of the soil and exercising collective rights of ownership in the lands of their mark. In this " paradise of yeomen " the free husbandman is judged only in the court of the mark, submits to the customs of the mark alone, acknowledges no other head but the " first markman," hereditary or elected, or the powerful warrior who secures the safety of the mark. This head, however, ends, thanks to his prerogatives and usurpations, by reducing the members of the community to economic dependence. The lands not yet exploited, which should have remained as a reserve fund at the disposal of the people, fall into the hands of the chief men. This capital phenomenon fully explains the formation of the feudal and manorial system.[2]

Kemble had the merit of raising questions which are still debated at the present day; unfortunately, his

The Mark theory has been partially abandoned. structure is a creation of fancy. Maurer, on the contrary, founded his Mark theory on a thorough study of the German village of the Middle Ages. But Fustel de Coulanges has accused him of having " attributed to ancient Germany

1. A summary of this controversy may be found in Vinogradoff, *Villainage in England,* pp. 16 sqq.; C. M. Andrews, *Old English Manor* (Baltimore, 1892) *Introduction*; E. A. Bryan, *The Mark in Europe and America* (Berlin, 1893), etc.

2. Kemble, *Saxons in England,* ed. W. de Gray Birch, 1876, vol. i, especially pp. 53 sqq., 176 sqq.

usages whose existence can only be verified twelve
centuries later,"[1] and has partly succeeded in over-
throwing the "mark-system." The Germanists can no
longer maintain that the mark is " the original basis on
which all Teutonic societies are founded,"[2] and even
Stubbs, who appears to be unacquainted with the works
of Fustel, and quotes those of Maurer with unqualified
praise, makes some prudent reservations. He does not
admit that the mark is a " fundamental constitutional
element." But he thinks that the English village
" represents the principle of the mark," and in the pages
which he devotes to the township and the manor, he
allows no place to Roman or Celtic influences.[3] The
majority of the best-known English historians of his
generation and ours, Henry Sumner Maine, Freeman,
Green, Maitland,[4] are, like him, decided Germanists. In
the same camp are ranged the German scholars who
have studied or approached the problem of the origin
of English civilization on any side, such as Konrad
Maurer, Nasse, Gneist and Meitzen.

Until 1883, the Romanists had not given uneasiness
to the English scholars of the Germanist school. The
The Romanists. work of Coote[5] was built in the air, on
analogies and suppositions which were
often extravagant; it is difficult to take seriously his
theories on the fiscal survey of the whole of Britain, on
the persistence of the Roman *Comes* and on the Roman
origin of the shire. The book in which Fustel de

1. *De la marche germanique* in *Recherches sur quelques problèmes d'histoire*, 1885, p. 356. Cf. *Le problème des origines de la propriété foncière*, in *Questions Historiques*, ed. Jullian, 1893, p. 21 sqq.

2. Kemble, *Saxons*, p. 53.

3. *Const. Hist.*, i, pp. 35 sqq., 52 sqq., 89 sqq., 97 sqq. For Stubbs' general views on the Germanic origin of English institutions, see *ibid.* pp. 2 sqq., 65, 68.

4. Mr. Maitland, however, entirely rejects the term 'mark' as applicable to the English village community. See *Domesday Book and Beyond*, pp. 354–355.

5. *The Romans of Britain*, 1878.

Coulanges had studied Roman Gaul was little known on the other side of the Channel; nor would it have shaken the conviction of scholars who consider that English institutions have had an absolutely original development and are the " purest product of the primitive genius of the Germans." In 1883, the famous work of Mr. F. Seebohm appeared to disturb the tranquillity of the Germanists.

Mr. Seebohm set himself to examine " The English Village Community in its relations to the manorial and tribal systems and to the common or open field system of husbandry." Such was the title of the book; the problem to be solved was indicated in the preface thus : " whether the village communities of England were originally free and this liberty degenerated into serfdom, or whether they were at the dawn of history in serfdom under the authority of a lord, and the ' manor ' already in existence."

The author proceeds from the known to the unknown; his starting point is a description of the remains of open field cultivation which he has himself observed in England. He has no difficulty in proving that this system was already employed at the end of the Middle Ages, and co-existed with the manorial organisation and villeinage. He then goes back to the period of the Norman Conquest. According to him, when the Normans arrived in England, they brought with them no new principle in the management of estates. Already, *tempore regis Edwardi,* we find the manor, with a lord's demesne and a village community composed of serfs, whom the lord has provided with indivisible holdings; the Domesday Book of the eastern counties speaks indeed of *liberi homines* and *sochemanni,* but they were Danes or Normans : the natives were not free tenants. Earlier still, in the time of King Ine or Ini, at the end of the seventh century, the usages of the open field existed, the *ham* and the *tun* were manors, the *thegn*

or *hlaford* was the lord of a manor, the *ceorl* was a serf.
And as in the laws of Ethelbert a century older, there
is mention of *hams* or *tuns* belonging to private
individuals or to the king, the manor must already have
existed at the end of the sixth century.   Now, the
Anglo-Saxons, at that time, had scarcely completed the
conquest of the island; it is impossible, therefore, that
the free village community, conforming to the mark
system, can have been introduced by them into England,
since the first documents that we have on their social
condition prove that this free community did not exist.
Therefore either the Saxons brought the system of the
manor and the servile community into England, or else
they found it already established there, and made no
change in it.   This second hypothesis is

**The manor
and villeinage
of Roman
origin.**
the more probable; the manorial and servile
organisation must go back to the period of
Roman domination in Britain.   It will be
objected that the Romans were few in number, that the
Britons were Celts, and that, in the countries where
Celtic civilization persisted, Wales and Ireland, the
manorial organisation did not exist in the Middle Ages.
The Celtic tribal community was entirely unacquainted
with the fixed and indivisible holding which is
one of the essential features of the manor.   But,
declares Mr. Seebohm, there is nothing to prove that
before the arrival of the Anglo-Saxons the whole of
Britain was still under the empire of the customs of
pastoral and tribal civilization.   The evidence of Cæsar
proves that the inhabitants of the south-east had already
passed out of this stage.   The Romans found subjects
accustomed to a settled life.   They had no difficulty in
establishing in their new province the régime of the
' villa,' the great estate, that is to say, the manor : and
the administrative abuses of the Lower Empire hastened
the formation of the seignorial authority and the
enslavement of the free husbandmen, Germans for the

most part, whom the emperors had imported in large numbers to colonise the country. The Romans, for the rest, improved agriculture and introduced the use of the triple rotation of crops; they thus gave to the open field system, which the Britons had only practised until then in its most rudimentary form, its definitive constitution.

As for the hypothesis according to which the open field system with triple rotation and lordship with servile, indivisible holdings, was introduced after the fall of the Roman domination, by the Anglo-Saxons, it is not indefensible, but only upon condition that the Anglo-Saxons came from Southern Germany, which had undergone contact with Roman civilization, and not, as is generally thought, from Northern Germany, where the triple rotation of crops was unknown. Mr. Seebohm does not reject this supposition, which, indeed, does not exclude the first hypothesis. Half Romanised Germans may have found in England the system of husbandry with which they were already acquainted on the Continent. In either case the English manor has a Roman origin.

Mr. Seebohm's work compels attention by the skill with which the author sets forth his ideas and puts fresh **Objections.** life into the subject. As we shall see, it has obliged the Germanists to make important concessions. But the theory, taken as a whole, is untenable. We are struck, in reading it, by the viciousness of his general method, by the missing links in **The Roman** his chain of proof, by the poverty of many **origin is not** of his arguments. The method of working **proved.** back adopted by Mr. Seebohm is extremely fallacious; it falsifies the historical perspective, and the author is inevitably led to reason in most cases by analogy. By such a method, if some day the documents of modern history disappear bodily, a scholar might undertake to connect the trades unions of the nineteenth century with the Roman *Collegia.* " No amount of analogy between two systems," says Stubbs wisely, " can by itself prove the actual derivation of one from the other."[1]

Mr. Seebohm juggles with texts and centuries very adroitly, but not by any means enough to create the illusion of continuity which he claims to see himself in going back through the course of the ages. There are yawning gaps in his demonstration.

The alleged proof drawn from the laws of Ethelbert amounts to nothing; the thesis of a Roman England entirely divided into great estates is an absurd improbability; the same is true of the supposition that the Saxon pirates could have come from the centre of Europe. Even when Mr. Seebohm treads on ground which appears more solid, and quotes his documents, he is unconvincing. In fact, from the time that he arrives, in his backward march, at Domesday Book, he loses hold on realities and allows himself to be duped by his fixed idea. He is the sport of a veritable historical mirage, when he sees the whole of England in the eleventh century, covered with manors like those of the thirteenth and cultivated by serfs. Still more misleading is the illusion by which England presents itself to him under the same aspect during the Anglo-Saxon period. According to him, the ceorl is a serf; he is the conquered native; the Saxon conquerors are the lords of manors, the successors of great Roman landowners. He takes no account of the texts which prove the freedom of the ceorl, and the existence of the small landholder; he does not explain at all what became of the mass of the German immigrants who had crossed the North Sea in sufficient numbers to impose their language on the Britons. His mistake is as huge as that of Boulainvilliers, who sought the origin of the French nobility and of feudalism in the supremacy of the Frank conquerors and the subjection of the Gallo-Romans.

1. Stubbs, *op. cit.* i, p. 227.

Mr. Seebohm's Romanist thesis, despite a brilliant success in the book market, has, in short, turned out but a spent shot. Among English historians of mark Mr. Ashley now stands alone, and with many reservations too, as its defender.[1] But it has had the merit of stimulating the critical spirit and of inducing the moderate Germanists, such as Green or Mr. Vinogradoff, to make concessions which we think justified.

There is, in fact, no necessity to range oneself in either camp, to be " Germanist " or " Romanist," to **The true method.** neglect completely, as Stubbs has set the regrettable example of doing, all facts anterior to the Germanic conquest, or to fall, like Coote or Mr. Seebohm, into the opposite extreme.

It is not reasonable to seek a single origin for English institutions, and to pretend to explain by one formula a very complex state of things, which was bound to vary not only in time, but also in space. The eclectic method adopted by Mr. Vinogradoff in his recent work on the " Origin of the Manor," appears to us a very judicious one, and we believe it alone to be capable of leading to the real solution.

To begin with, room must certainly be left for an original element which the uncompromising Germanists **The Celtic element.** and Romanists alike have, by common consent, ruled out of the discussion : the Celtic element.[2]

1. *The origin of Property in Land*, by Fustel de Coulanges, translated by Margaret Ashley, with an introductory chapter on the English Manor, by W. J. Ashley, 1891; 2nd edition, 1892.—*An introduction to English Economic History*, vol. 1, 3rd edition, 1894, translated by P. Bondois and corrected by the author, under the title of *Hist. des doctrines économiques de l'Angleterre*, 1900, vol. i, pp. 30 sqq.

2. We do not mean to say that England, before the arrival of the Romans and Germans, was peopled by Celts only. There were pre-Celtic populations, perhaps more important as regards numbers, but the Celtic civilization predominated. See a very interesting general sketch of the English races in H. J. Mackinder, *Britain and the British Seas*, 1902, pp. 179 sqq. A summary bibliography of works relative to the Prehistoric and Celtic periods will be found in Gross, *Sources and Literature of English History*, 1900, pp. 157 sqq.

We can get an approximate idea of its character and creative action,—on condition of being content with general conclusions,—by consulting the much later and indirect sources which we possess on Celtic tribal civilization : the Welsh laws especially, the Irish laws, and the information we have on the Scottish clan, or on the Celts of the Continent.[1]

Whatever Mr. Seebohm may say, it is allowable to believe that the Britons, as Pytheas or even Cæsar knew them,[2] had not passed, from an economic point of view, the stage of tribal and still semi-pastoral civilization. Judging by the general history of the Celts and the data of comparative history, they knew nothing similar to the manor. The inferior class called *taeogs* dwelt apart, and did not work for the benefit of the free men. There was neither servile tenure nor even private property in the strict sense of the word. Their principal resource was cattle-rearing; Celtic agriculture was an extensive superficial agriculture, which required neither careful work, nor capital for the improvement of the soil. It was little fitted to inspire the feeling of individual proprietorship.

On the other hand the method of labour required the spirit of co-operation. The plough was large and heavy; eight oxen were usually yoked to it; it was so costly a thing that it could only belong to a group of persons, and it is for this reason that, according to the Welsh laws, the land was divided into parcels assigned to the members of each plough-association, one supplying the plough-share, others the oxen, others undertaking to plough and lead the team.[3] An understanding between

Origin of the Open Field.

Marginalia: The open field system was Celtic. The Britons were a tribal, pastoral people, with extensive, superficial agricultural system. Their agriculture was co-operative.

1. For all that follows, cf. Vinogradoff, *Growth of the Manor*, pp. 3 sqq.

2. For the fragments of the journal of Pytheas, preserved in various ancient authors, and for Cæsar's description, see J. Rhys, *Celtic Britain*, 2nd edition, 1884, pp. 5 sqq., 53 sqq.

3. Seebohm, *English Village Community*, pp. 122 sqq.

the workers being indispensable for ploughing, and individual effort being reduced to a minimum, the conception of private property could not be the same as with our peasantry. The assignation of shares by lot, and the frequent redistribution of these shares were quite

Idea of property

natural things. Finally, the great importance of sheep and cattle rearing, of hunting and fishing was very apt to preserve communist habits. Everything inclines us to believe that in England the English village community and the open field system have their roots in the Celtic tribal civilization.[1]

This probability cannot be rejected unless it can be proved that the Britons were exterminated and their agricultural usages completely rooted out, either by the Romans or by the Anglo-Saxons; and that is a thing which is impossible of proof.

The Romans did not exterminate the Britons, and recent archæological excavations appear to prove that

The Roman element.

the manner of living of the native lower classes, their way of constructing their villages and of burying their dead, remained quite unaffected by contact with Roman civilization.[2]

Many regions of Britain entirely escaped this contact, none underwent it very thoroughly. The emperors' chief care was to occupy Britain in a military sense, in order to protect Gaul, and its foggy climate attracted few immigrants.[3]

1. I do not claim, it must be understood, that primitively the open field was peculiar to the Celts. Mr. Vinogradoff is of opinion that the system originated in habits of husbandry common to all the peoples of the North (*Growth of the Manor*, p. 106, Note 58). Mr. Gomme likewise thinks that the village community existed among all the Aryan peoples (*The Village Community*, 1890). This goes to show that these institutions had not been brought into England by foreigners, within historical times.

2. See A. H. L. F. Pitt Rivers, *Excavations in Cranborne Chase*, 1887—1898.

3. These characteristics of the Roman occupation are very well brought out and explained by Green, *Making of England*, 5th edition, 1900, pp. 5 sqq. Mr. Haverfield somewhat exaggerates the Romanisation of

Still the Roman domination lasted for three and a half centuries on the other side of the Channel, and every year English archæologists bring to light some comfortable or luxurious villa, with pavements in mosaic, painted stucco, hypocausts and baths.[1]

Evidently the Roman officials, like the English in India to-day, knew how to make themselves comfortable;

The Villa. they brought with them industries and arts which pleased the higher ranks of the Britons. And this at least must be retained out of the hazardous theories of Mr. Seebohm, that the estate organised on the Italian model, the great landowner living in a fine country house, having the part he had reserved for himself cultivated by slaves, and letting out the rest of his property to *coloni,* were by no means unknown in Britain. By the side of the free Britons grouped in communities, there was a landed aristocracy.

The disturbance caused by the German conquest, by the wholesale immigration of the Angles and Saxons was no doubt immense. Stubbs is justified

The Anglo-Saxon element. in appealing to the philological argument : the fact that the Celtic and Latin languages disappeared before Anglo-Saxon is sufficient to prove how thoroughly England was Germanised. But Stubbs is mistaken in looking upon England at the arrival of the Germans as a *tabula rasa.* What he calls the 'Anglo-Saxon system ' was not built up on ground that was levelled and bare. It was the interest of the conquerors

Britain in the *Introductory Sketch of Roman Britain,* printed at the beginning of the excellent studies which he has written for the *Victoria History of the Counties of England;* for instance, in the *Victoria History of Hampshire,* vol. i, 1900. The publication is announced of a general work by that scholar, entitled, *The Romanisation of Roman Britain.* Cf. on the Roman occupation; Vinogradoff, *Growth of the Manor,* pp. 37 sqq., and the chapter by Mr. Thomas Hodgkin, in vol. i of the *Political History of England,* edited by W. Hunt and R. L. Poole, 1906, pp. 52 sqq.

1. See Mr. Haverfield's studies : *Victoria History of Hampshire,* vol. i, 1900; *Worcester,* vol. i, 1901; *Norfolk,* vol. i, 1901; *Northamptonshire,* vol. i, 1902; *Warwickshire,* vol. i, 1904; *Derbyshire,* vol. i, 1905, etc.

to utilise the remains of Roman civilization. Nor is it by
Persistence of the earlier agrarian customs. any means proved that where they settled they exterminated the native population.[1]
They had no aversion to the usages of the open field, and could quickly accustom themselves to live side by side with the British peasants. The Celtic tribal communities would be absorbed in the village communities formed by the *ceorls*. At the same time, the very great inequality which prevailed among the Anglo-Saxons, the development of royal dynasties and ealdorman families richly endowed with land, and, lastly, the grants made to the Church, necessarily preserved the great estate, cultivated with the help of ' theows ' or slaves and of *coloni*.

Nevertheless, for the establishment of the seignorial system in England it was not enough that there were
Tendencies towards a new classification of society. rich men and ' theows.' The predominance of the small freehold, the existence of numerous ' ceorls ' cultivating their hide[2] and members of independent communities,
were incompatible with the general establishment of the manorial system. A new classification of

---

1. J. Rhys, *Celtic Britain*, pp. 109–110. See also R. A. Smith in the *Victoria History of Hampshire*, vol. i, p. 376; he gives the bibliography of the question.

2. The hide has been the subject of numberless controversies. There is a whole literature on the question, and the subject is not exhausted, for the good reason that the term has several meanings, and the hide was not, as a matter of fact, a fixed measure. Stubbs states that the hide of the Norman period "was no doubt a hundred and twenty or a hundred acres" (*Const. Hist.*, i, p. 79). But he should have drawn a distinction between the fiscal hide, which was a unit of taxation, and the real or field hide. Mr. Round (*Feudal England*, 1895, pp. 36 sqq.; see also *Victoria History of Bedfordshire*, 1904, vol. i, pp. 191—193) and Professor Maitland (*Domesday Book and Beyond*, pp. 357 sqq.) have shown the artificial character of the Domesday hide. This hide was very generally divided into 120 fractions called acres [for fiscal hides of fewer acres see Vinogradoff, *Growth of the Manor*, p. 155], but these appellations did not correspond to any fixed reality, any more than did the "ploughland" (*carrucata*) and the "sulung" or the French "hearths" of the Middle Ages. The *hide* (or *hiwisc, hiwship*), in its other sense, the primitive one, which it continued to retain alongside its fiscal sense, denoted the quantity (obviously variable according to locality) of

society had to come into existence; some freemen had to *great estates in-* descend in the social scale, while others raised them- *creased by royal* selves. This transformation was inevitable in an age in *grants, commen-* which the old bonds of tribe and family no longer *dation, etc.* sufficed to give security to the individual, and in which the royal power was not yet able to ensure it. Throughout Christendom patronage and commendation, along with private appropriation of public powers, paved the way for a new political and social system.

The Anglo-Saxon kings, under the pressure of necessities which were not peculiar to them, at an early

Gifts of land and royal rights to thegns and churches. period bestowed on their thegns and on churches either lands or the rights which they possessed over some village and the community of freemen who dwelt there. Thenceforward such thegns or churches levied on their own account the taxes, dues and supplies hitherto due to the king; for example, the profitable *firma unius noctis*. Armed with this right the recipient

Commendation. became the lord of the free village, the peasants commended themselves to him,[1] and the parcel of land or the house which he possessed in the neighbourhood became a centre of manorial organisation; the lands of the peasants who had commended themselves came ultimately to be considered as in some way held of him. The grant of judicial rights

Sac and Soc. (*sac and soc*) was also a powerful instrument of subjection. When a church or thegn received a grant of sac and soc in a district the rights

arable land and rights of common necessary for the maintenance of a family. The actual number of acres in the real hide was often 120, but not always. The hide is not therefore an agrarian measure; it is the unit of landed property, the *terra familiae*, and we must doubtless conclude that the hundred was an aggregation of a hundred of these hides. See Vinogradoff, *Growth of the Manor*, pp. 141, 151 sqq., 170, 250, Note 33. Stubbs says elsewhere (*op. cit.* p. 185) that "the hide is the provision of a family." He ought to have adhered to that definition.

1. On Anglo-Saxon commendation, see Maitland, *Domesday Book and Beyond*, p. 69; Pollock and Maitland, *History of English Law*, vol. i, pp. 30, 31.

so conferred were exercised, either in the court of the hundred or in whatever popular court it pleased the grantee to set up; the reeve of the church or thegn presided over the court and received the fines. Stubbs ascribes the beginning of grants of sac and soc to the reign of Canute; but Mr. Maitland makes them go back to the seventh century.[1]

The evolution which was carrying England towards the seignorial régime became a very much speedier **Results of the struggle against the Danes.** process in consequence of the struggles against the Danes in the ninth and tenth centuries. Professional soldiers, expensively armed, were alone capable of arresting this new wave of barbarians, and they necessarily became privileged persons. Military service was henceforth the obligation and attribute of thegns. Most of them had at least five hides, that is to say, landed property five times as large as the old normal family holding, and the revenue of their estates allowed them, with the serjeants whom they maintained (*geneats, radknights, drengs*) to devote themselves entirely to the profession of arms. A deeply defined division began to show itself **Military and landed aristocracy.** between these thegns or *twelfhynd-men* and the simple *ceorls* or *twyhynd-men*,[2] who continued to till the land and lost their old warlike character, that is to say, their best title to the privileges of a freeman. There remained soldiers on the one hand and tillers of the soil on the other. Labour in the fields had been formerly the occupation of every freeman; it was henceforward a sign of inferiority. At the same time the old tradition of the inalienable family holding grew weaker, many of the ceorls no longer had the hide necessary for maintaining a household and the

1. Maitland, *Domesday Book and Beyond*, pp. 80 sqq., 226 sqq., 236 sqq., 258 sqq., 318 sqq.; Vinogradoff, *Growth of the Manor*, pp. 212 sqq.

2. On the meaning of the terms *twelfhynd-men* and *twyhynd-men*, see below, pp. 36 sqq.

virgate, the quarter of a hide[1] became the common type of small freehold. To escape calamity therefore men were obliged to abase themselves before some powerful neighbour. Little by little, for reasons at once economic and political, the bonds of dependence were drawn closer between the " liber pauper " and the thegn, rich, esteemed, endowed by the king with a portion of public authority, and become, as it were, his responsible representative in the district.[2] This formation of a military and landed aristocracy is a general phenomenon in the history of the West, which explains, in France as in England, the decay of the small freeholders and the definitive entrance of the seignorial system.

Domesday Book, drawn up twenty years after the Norman invasion, allows us to form some idea of the state of rural England at the end of the Anglo-Saxon period. It is a document bristling with difficulties, and of baffling obscurity. But, since the appearance of the 'Constitutional History,' it has been the subject of a number of admirable studies, some of which were known to Stubbs and might have been utilised more by him in the last editions of his work. Mr. Round has elucidated some particularly thorny questions in his *Feudal England,* and he and other scholars are at present furnishing the editors of the *Victoria History of the Counties of England* with a detailed examination, county by county, of all the historical information that *Domesday Book* contains. Mr. Maitland has drawn a masterly picture of Anglo-Saxon society in the eleventh century in his *Domesday Book and Beyond,* an at times daring but extremely suggestive synthesis, one of the finest books which

The England of Domesday Book

1. On the virgate, see Vinogradoff, *Villainage,* p. 239; J. Tait, *Hides and virgates at Battle Abbey,* in *English Historical Review,* xviii, 1903, pp. 705 sqq.

2. Maitland, *Domesday Book,* pp. 163 sqq.; Vinogradoff, *Growth of the Manor,* pp. 216 sqq.; A. G. Little, *Gesiths and Thegns,* in *English Historical Review,* iv, 1889, pp. 723 sqq.

B

English scholarship has produced. Finally Mr. Vinogradoff, in his *Villainage in England* and his quite recent *Growth of the Manor* [and *English Society in the Eleventh Century*], has put forth solutions which deserve the most favourable attention.

The very nature of the document, the end King William had in view in commanding this great inquest, are sufficiently mysterious to begin with. For Mr. Round and Mr. Maitland, Domesday is a fiscal document, a " Geld-Book " designed to facilitate an equitable imposition of the Danegeld. Mr. Vinogradoff reverts to an older and more comprehensive definition, and believes that the royal commissioners wished not only to prepare the way for the collection of the tax, but also to discriminate the ties which united the subjects of the king to one another, and to know, from one end of England to the other, from whom each piece of land was held; in this way alone the political and administrative responsibilities of the lords in their relation to the king could be fixed.[1] We now understand why England, as the commissioners describe it, seems to be already divided into manors. Mr. Seebohm allowed himself to be misled by this appearance.[2] In reality the agents of the king spoke of manors where there were none, where there was nothing but a piece of land with a barn, capable of becoming some day a centre of manorial organisation; for it was of importance for the schemes of the Norman monarchy that the seignorial system should be extended everywhere.

Difficulties of interpretation

1. *Growth of the Manor*, pp. 292 sqq.
2. Mr. Maitland, on the contrary, puts into sharp relief the contrast which exists between the manor of *Domesday Book* and the manor of the 13th century. He concludes that the manor of *Domesday* is not the seignorial estate, but the place at which the geld is received (*Domesday Book and Beyond*, pp. 119 sqq.). This theory is untenable. See J. Tait, in *English Historical Review*, xii, 1897, pp. 770—772; Round, *ibidem*, xv, 1900, pp. 293 sqq. *Victoria History of Hampshire*, i, 443, *Victoria History of Bedfordshire*, i, 210; Lapsley, *Vict. Hist. of Durham*, i, 260; Salzmann, *Vict. Hist. of Sussex*, i, 355; Vinogradoff, *Growth of the Manor*, pp. 300 sqq.

Moreover, the nomenclature used is a source of perplexity and mistakes; the compilers often use Norman terms; the names they choose sometimes change their meaning later, so much so that they have become subject of controversy amongst modern scholars.

The difficulty, then, of an exact interpretation of *Domesday Book* is great. And even when the necessary
Social complexity precautions have been taken, it is a peculiarly arduous task to elicit from the document a clear description of Anglo-Saxon society *tempore regis Edwardi*.

Stubbs shows well how extraordinary was its complexity, what variety the ties created by commendation and gifts of land presented, and how diverse the personal and territorial relations were. The small freehold still existed side by side with the great estate; the most populous region, the Danelaw,[1] was a country of free husbandmen, of village communities.[2] Not only were there lands which belonged neither to thegns nor to churches, but there were, in the England of Edward the Confessor, whole villages, and in large numbers, in which the fiscal and judicial rights of the king had not fallen into private hands, nor did such villages form part of the royal demesne properly so called.

Ties of Dependence But the free husbandmen were for all that involved in the ties of dependence, as, indeed, were their lords, for the thegns were themselves thegns of an ealdorman, or a church, or another thegn, or the queen, or the king.[3]

The free village existed beside the manor in the time of Domesday.

---

1. On the extent of the Danelaw or Danish district, see a note of Mr. Hodgkin, in the *Political History of England*, edited by R. L. Poole and W. Hunt, i, 1906, pp. 315—317 [and Chadwick, *Anglo-Saxon Institutions*, p. 198].

2. Mr. Maitland remarks on the need of guarding against the temptation that assails those who have read *Domesday Book*, to see great estates everywhere at the end of the Anglo-Saxon period (*Domesday Book and Beyond*, pp. 64, 168 sqq.).

3. Maitland, *Domesday Book*, p. 162. Upon the *láen-lands* granted by the Church to the thegns, see *ibidem*, pp. 301 sqq.

The same personal or territorial ties which attached the members of the military aristocracy to one another established infinitely varied relations between them and the rest of the free population. The *liberi homines commendatione tantum* could leave their lord when they wished, for they had not subjected their land to him, and they had the right to " recedere cum terra sua absque licentia domini sui."[1] Sometimes, on the other hand, the *commendatio* attached the land to the lord, and if the land was sold, it remained under the commendation of the same lord. In certain cases the land belongs to a *soc*, and he who buys it has to recognise the judicial rights of the lord. Finally, the freeman may hold a *terra consuetudinaria* and owe dues or agricultural services; such are the *sochemanni cum omni consuetudine*[2] in the eastern counties, whom the compilers of *Domesday Book* would have called *villani* in another part of England.[3]

This last expression has been the source of mistaken theories which Messrs. Maitland and Vinogradoff have

The villeins of Domesday Book

fully succeeded in clearing out of the way. In the eyes of Mr. Seebohm especially all the *villani* of *Domesday Book* were villeins in the sense which the word acquired later on in England, that is, peasants subject to personal servitude.[4] In reality, the term has no legal sense here; *villanus* is the translation of *tunesman,* man of the village; he is, according to Mr. Vinogradoff, a member of the village community, who possesses the normal share in the open field. He has the same wergild as the *sochemannus*

---

1. See the numerous passages quoted by Round, *Feudal England*, pp. 24 sqq.

2. *Ibidem*, pp. 31 sqq.

3. On the sokemen of *Domesday Book*, see Maitland. *Domesday Book and Beyond*, pp. 66, 104 sqq.; Vinogradoff, *Manor*, p. 341; [*English Society*, pp. 124, 431.]

4. *English Village Community*, pp. 89—104. In his *Tribal Custom in Anglo-Saxon Law*, 1902. p. 504, Mr. Seebohm begs that this servitude may not be confounded with slavery.

and, like him, owes only agricultural services fixed by custom and very light; by the side of the land he holds from a lord he may have an independent holding. <u>In a general way at least, the *villein* of *Domesday* is a free man, a descendant of the ceorl, the twyhynd-man.</u>[1]

This social state, further complicated by the persistence of slavery, was the natural product of very remote

The Norman element antecedents, the fruit of the development and friction of several superimposed races, the spontaneous and varied result of the necessities of daily life and local historic forces, in a country where the pressure of the central power was extremely feeble. Neither the adventurers who followed William the Bastard in order to obtain a fine ' guerdon,' nor the servants of the Norman monarchy were disposed to respect this composite and bizarre edifice on which so many centuries had left their mark. They left standing only what was useful to them or did not inconvenience them. The Norman Conquest, begun by brutal soldiers and completed by jurists of orderly and logical mind, was to have for its effect the systematizing of the social grouping and its simplification at the expense of the weakest.

In fact and in law, the most original features of Anglo-Saxon society disappeared. In fact, during the hard

Result of the conquest for the native rural classes years which followed the landing of William the natives who were not massacred or expelled from their dwellings[2] had to

[margin handwritten note: The Norman conquerors imposed their own terms on the natives.]

---

1. Maitland, *op. cit.* pp. 38 sqq.; Vinogradoff, *Manor*, pp. 339 sqq. Mr. Maitland remarks also, with reason, that the conception of personal liberty is extremely difficult to fix in this period and throughout the whole of the Middle Ages; cf. the remarks of Stubbs (*Const. Hist.*, i, 83). See also Seebohm, *Tribal Custom*, p. 430.

2. Here is an example of the expulsion of a humble peasant : "Ricardus de Tonebrige tenet de hoc manerio unam virgatam cum silva unde abstulit rusticum qui ibi manebat" (*Domesday*, quoted by Maitland, *op. cit.* p. 61, note 5). The difficulty is to know if these cases, which cannot all have been mentioned in Domesday, were numerous. Stubbs has preferred to discuss this difficult question of the spoliation of the Anglo-Saxon proprietors, and the transfer of their lands to the companions of the Conqueror, only incidentally and without dwelling upon it. To what

accept the conquerors' terms. The small freeholders were reduced to a subordinate condition. The lands they held without being accountable for them to anyone were given

degree were the native English deprived of their estates? What were the new families which were established in England? At the time when Stubbs wrote his book, *Domesday Book* had perhaps not been studied enough for it to be possible to reply to questions like these. Stubbs speaks with great reserve while giving proof of his habitual perspicacity. Augustin Thierry believed in an expropriation *en masse*, without however basing his thesis on serious arguments. Reacting against this view, Freeman claimed that a large number of natives kept their lands; as is well known, he generally tries to reduce to a minimum the results of the Norman Conquest. Stubbs notes (vol. i, p. 281, note 2) the confiscation with which William punished the declared partisans of Harold, and quotes on that head the passage in the *Dialogus de Scaccario* (i, c. x; ed. Hughes, etc., p. 100); but he does not believe that the bulk of the small owners were dispossessed. "The actual amount of dispossession was greatest in the higher ranks; the smaller owners to a large extent remained in a mediatised position on their estates." Mr. Round, in the studies which the *Victoria History* is at present publishing, hesitates to formulate a very decided opinion on this difficult subject; but he rejects the view of Freeman more completely than does Stubbs : "So far as we can judge all but a few specially favoured individuals were deprived of the lands they had held, or at most were allowed to retain a fragment or were placed in subjection to a Norman lord. And even the exceptions, there is reason to believe, were further reduced after Domesday" (*Victoria Hist. of Bedfordshire*, i, 1904, pp. 206–207). He confesses elsewhere that "great obscurity still surrounds the process by which the English holders were dispossessed by the strangers. The magnates, no doubt, were dispossessed either at the opening of William's reign or, on various pretexts, in the course of it" (*Vict. Hist. of Warwickshire*, i, 1904, p. 282). Mr. Round, it is obvious, does not believe in an immediate and methodical dispossession, but he considers that the cases in which an Englishman was fortunate enough to escape the storm were rare. Certain natives, like Oda of Winchester, particularly favoured by the Conqueror, lost their old estates and received others in their place : "In this, no doubt, there was deep policy; for they would henceforth hold by his own grant alone, and would be led, moreover, to support his rule against the English holders they had dispossessed" (*Vict. Hist. of Hampshire*, i, 1900, pp. 427–428. See also *Essex*, i, 1903, pp. 354–355; *Buckinghamshire*, i, 1905, p. 217). Saving these not very numerous exceptions, the Conquest, in Mr. Round's opinion, was a great misfortune for all the English. Let us remark that it is necessary to distinguish between the counties, and that on the borders of the kingdom, dispossession was more difficult. Mr. W. Farrer (*Victoria Hist. of Lancashire*, i, 1906, 283) considers that, in the region which under Henry II became the county of Lancaster, the greater number of the manors were held in the 12th century by descendants of the old Anglo-Saxon owners. With regard to the families from the Continent who were endowed with lands in England, many new details and rectifications will be found in Mr. Round's articles. He rightly insists in the pages he devotes to Northamptonshire, that the conquerors were far from being all Normans; in Northamptonshire, there were many Flemings and Picards (*Vict. History of Northamptonshire*, i, 1902, pp. 289 sqq.).

to Norman lords, and they could only continue to cultivate
them by submitting to an oppressive system of dues and
services; the same heavy burdens, of course, pressed
upon the estates formerly held in dependence on a thegn,
where rents and services had still been light.[1]

Domesday Book shows us a certain Ailric, who had a
fine estate of four hides, now obliged to hold it at farm
from a Norman lord, " graviter et miserabiliter;" [2]
it speaks of free men forcibly incorporated in a manor,
" ad perficiendum manerium," [3] of the creation of new
dues and the augmentation of the old. The diminu-
tion in the number of the *sochemanni* in the first twenty
years of William's reign is characteristic : in the county
of Cambridge there are no more than 213 of them
instead of 900; 700 have descended to an inferior social
rank.[4] In the county of Hertford the decadence of this
class is equally striking.[5] In short, small free ownership
has received a mortal blow, and the anarchy of Stephen's
reign will complete the founding of the seignorial or
manorial system.[6]

In law, the legal theory of ownership changed. All
land, outside the royal demesne, was held of some one,
was a tenement, that is, the subject of a
New theory of ownership. Tenure dependent tenure, and the principle of
" no land without a lord " was intro-
duced into England. In addition every tenure involved

1. Upon the whole of this question and upon the arguments drawn
from the later condition of the peasants of the Ancient Demesne of
the Crown and of Kent, see Maitland, *Domesday Book*, pp. 60 sqq.; Vino
gradoff, *Villainage*, pp. 89 sqq., 205 sqq.; *Growth of the Manor*, pp.
295 sqq., 316 sqq.

2. Passage quoted by Maitland, *op. cit.* p. 61, note 3.

3. *Ibidem*, pp. 127–128.

4. *Ibidem*, pp. 62, 63. On these statistics of *Domesday*, see Maitland,
op. cit. p. 17 ; Round, *Victoria History of Hampshire*, i, p. 433.

5. Round, in *Victoria History of Hertfordshire*, i, 1902, pp. 265 sqq.

6. On the troubles of Stephen's reign, see Stubbs, *Const. Hist.* i, 353
sqq.; H. W. C. Davis, *The Anarchy of Stephen's reign*, in *English
Historical Review*, xviii, 1903, pp. 630 sqq. Vinogradoff, *Villainage*, pp
218–219.

some service. The military class definitively constituted itself in England in the eleventh and twelfth centuries, based on the very simple rule that a fief carries with it service in the army. In the same way the peasants were all tenants owing dues and generally manual labour; the conditions of their tenure became the essential criterion of their social rank. The manifold distinctions which divide the rural population in the Anglo-Saxon period, and of which traces remain in *Domesday Book,* were effaced under the double pressure of the seignorial authority and the common law. Slavery, which was repugnant to the habits of the Normans, and was in no

Two kinds of rural tenure sort of harmony with the principles of manorial exploitation,[1] completely disappeared. In the thirteenth century there are on the land only freeholders, perhaps in small numbers,[2] and villeins. It is, above all, the burdens of tenure in villeinage which constitute villein status, and the legal presumption of villeinage; he is not free who performs for his lord a " servile work," such as manuring the land or cleaning the ditches.[3]

1. See Maitland, *Domesday Book,* pp. 35–36.

2. See the case of the manor of Wilburton in Mr. Maitland's monograph, *English Historical Review,* ix, 1894, p. 418.

3. It is true that, if we examine the legal and manorial records relative to villeinage, matters are not so simple. The lawyers considered the villein as in a state of personal servitude towards his lord. *Servus, nativus, villanus,* are the same thing. The villein belongs, body and chattels, to his lord, has not the right to leave him, must pay *merchetum* when he marries his daughter. The reason is that the villeins of the thirteenth century were not descended only from the ancient Anglo-Saxon ceorls, the *villani* of *Domesday Book,* free men whom the troubles of the times had compelled to enter into the manorial organisation, to accept an aggravation of dues and services; there were also many villeins descended from Anglo-Saxon slaves (*theows; serri* of *Domesday*). The villein class of the English Middle Ages sprang from this fusion. The Norman lord treated the ceorls burdened with labour-services and the theows alike; the theows gained thereby, but the ceorls lost; by contact with the slaves who became their equals they contracted some of the marks of servitude which degraded their companions, and the dying institution of slavery did not disappear without leaving stains behind it. Nevertheless, in practice, this personal servitude to which the villeins and not the freeholders are subject has no great importance. The conditions of tenure are the important thing. And here is a striking

For the rest, we must not exaggerate the difference which, in the thirteenth century, separated the tenant in villeinage and the tenant in socage.

Slight difference between these two kinds of tenure

From the economic point of view, their burdens differ in quality and quantity, but they are very nearly equivalent. From the point of view of the defence of his rights, the freeholder is protected by the royal courts, while the villein has generally no action against his lord; but, in fact, he is perfectly protected against arbitrary treatment by the custom of the manor. Finally, as we have seen, he forms part of the village community by the same title as the freeholder.[1]

We have thus arrived again at the point from which we started. We have seen how the masters of English mediæval scholarship reply just now to the questions we put to ourselves. Even if we put on one side those who claim to explain the problems of the manor, the open field, villeinage and the village community by a Romanist theory which certainly cannot be accepted, these historians are far from being in agreement on all points. Mr. Maitland is a Germanist after the manner of Stubbs; the internal development of Anglo-Saxon society seems to him to be the key to all these mysteries; he willingly recognises the effects of the great catastrophe of 1066; but, for him, the seignorial system already existed in England at the end of the

Conclusion

proof : the free peasants who have succeeded in not allowing themselves to be assimilated to the *servi*. the freeholders, or tenants in *socage*, are considered free as long as they have a free holding, burdened only with light and occasional services; if they accept a villein tenement, they come to be considered as serfs, personally dependent on their lord, pay the merchetum and are even called villeins, like the others. They can lawfully leave their holding, but they do not avail themselves of this right of renouncing their means of existence; and thus the tenement in villeinage imposes the status of a villein on him who takes it up. On the whole question, see Vinogradoff, *Villainage*, pp. 43 sqq., 127 sqq.; *Growth of the Manor*, pp. 296 sqq., 343 sqq.; Pollock and Maitland, *History of English Law*, 2nd edition, 1898, i, pp. 356 sqq.

1. Vinogradoff, *Villainage*, pp. 81 sqq., 308 sqq.

Saxon period, as well as feudalism. Mr. Round has not approached these great questions as a whole, and has only thrown light on certain aspects of them; without doubt he looks on them from an entirely different point of view to that of Mr. Maitland.[1]

Vinogradoff's theory summarized.

Finally, Mr. Vinogradoff refuses to begin the history of the English rural classes at the invasion of the Anglo-Saxon pirates. According to him, the village community and the customs of the open field had their roots in a distant antiquity, and maintained themselves without great change throughout all catastrophes, as very humble things, which do not inconvenience the conquerors and adapt themselves to their plans, can do. The pattern of the great manorial estate was set in England as early as the Roman period, but the 'manor' did not become general until very much later, as a result of the formation of a rich military aristocracy, which as early as the Anglo-Saxon period began to establish its economic and political dominance over the remainder of the freemen, and was replaced, after the Conquest of 1066, by the powerful Norman feudal baronage. With the triumph of the manorial system coincided perforce the disappearance of small free ownership and the appearance of villeinage.

This last solution is the one which we believe to conform most closely to the documents as a whole, to the data of general history, and to common sense. It is, nevertheless, only a provisional solution. It must be supported by more thorough and extensive study of documents, and it will be beyond all doubt rectified on more than one point. The question of the origin of the English village community particularly still remains very obscure. To resolve it, we must be better informed than we are about the Anglo-Saxon village. As Mr. Vinogradoff has remarked, its organisation was not changed by way of

Doubts concerning the village community

1. See *Feudal England*, p. 262.

legislation, and the modest concerns discussed by the
ceorls did not excite the curiosity of the historians of
that day, so that neither the laws nor the chronicles, give
us sufficient information on the rural community. It
existed undoubtedly; it watched over the collective concerns; but in what degree was it organised? Have we
any right to apply to the Anglo-Saxon township what we
know of the township of the thirteenth and fourteenth
centuries, as Mr. Vinogradoff has boldly done?[1]
Mr. Maitland advises caution, and without doubt he is
right. He remarks that the communal affairs that had
to be transacted in a free village were very few in number
and that many of these villages were very small.[2]

We do not know what influence the Norman Conquest
had upon the development of the rural communities.
Did it curtail their freedom, or, on the
other hand, did the Norman lords think it

The Norman
point of view

profitable to their interests to organise the
village more thoroughly? We must discuss the
question afresh, as Mr. Round, we shall see, has done
in the case of military tenure, placing ourselves at the
Norman point of view. English historians would do
well to give more serious attention to M. Leopold
Delisle's book on the agricultural class in Normandy.
It is well to remember that servitude disappeared very
early on the Norman estates; that the communities of
inhabitants " exercised most of the rights appertaining
to the true communes," that in the twelfth century some
of them had the services which their lord could demand
of them legally recognised, and that as early as the time
of William the Conqueror we see the peasants of
Benouville acting in a body and giving their church to
the nuns of the Trinity at Caen.[3] It would be desirable,

1. *Growth of the Manor*, p. 185 sqq.

2. *Domesday Book and Beyond*, pp. 20, 21, 148 sqq.

3. Delisle, *Etude sur la condition de la classe agricole en Normandie*,
1851, pp. 137 sqq.

also, to keep in mind that " the companions of William, in whom many people see nothing but the spoilers of the wealth of the Anglo-Saxons, in more than one way renewed the face of England. We must not forget that most of them were great agriculturists." [1]

1. *Ibid.*, p. 251.

II.

FOLKLAND.

Was there a " Public Land " among the Anglo-Saxons ?

Following Allen,[1] and along with all the scholars who have dealt with this question after Allen,[2] up to but

Mistake of Allen excluding Mr. Vinogradoff, Stubbs in the earlier editions of his book, gave to the Anglo-Saxon expression *folk-land* the meaning of " land of the people," *ager publicus,* and expounded a whole theory of this alleged institution. In 1893, Mr. Vinogradoff showed decisively that Allen was mistaken.[3] To this conclusive refutation Mr. Maitland, in 1897, added new arguments; he adopted, reproduced and completed it in a chapter of his *Domesday Book and Beyond.*[4]

Stubbs was evidently acquainted with the works of these two great jurists, although he does not expressly

Attitude of Stubbs quote them; in the last edition of his *Constitutional History* he alludes to the new explanation of the word *folkland,* given by " legal antiquaries," [5] and has even obviously altered some passages of his work, in which he spoke incidentally of

1. John Allen, *Inquiry into the rise and progress of the royal prerogative in England,* 1830; 2nd ed., 1849, pp. 125—153.

2. Kemble, Freeman, Thorpe, Lodge, Pollock, Gneist, Waitz, Sohm, Brunner, etc.

3. P. Vinogradoff, *Folkland* in *English Historical Review,* viii, 1893, pp. 1—17. Cf. Stubbs' somewhat ambiguous note (*Const. Hist.,* i, p. 81). See also Vinogradoff, *The Growth of the Manor,* 1905, pp. 142–143 and 244–245.

4. *Book-land and Folk-land,* in *Domesday Book and Beyond,* pp. 244–258.

5. Stubbs, i, p. 81, note 2.

folkland.[1] But his readers may ask themselves whether he accepts the opinion of Professors Vinogradoff and Maitland or no even as regards the meaning of the word. For, in several other passages, he lets the older interpretation of Allen [2] stand; elsewhere he tells us that " the change of learned opinion as to the meaning of *folkland* involves certain alterations in the terminology, but does not seem to militate against the idea of the public land;" [3] and he maintains his theory on the Anglo-Saxon *ager publicus,* when in reality it is impossible to admit its existence, if we adopt the conclusions of Mr. Vinogradoff on the meaning of the word folkland, as we are bound to do. An extraordinary confusion results from this hesitation of Stubbs, which, in view of the great and legitimate authority of the *Constitutional History,* will contribute to uphold a view of whose erroneousness there can be no doubt.[4]

It is important to warn readers of Stubbs that : (1) folkland does not mean public land; (2) that there was not in Anglo-Saxon England any " public land " distinct from the royal demesne.

The term *folkland* is to be found in three texts only; a law and two charters. According to a law of Edward the Elder (900—924 ?) it appears that all **Use of the word folkland** suits concerning landed property might be classed in two categories : suits regarding folkland, and suits regarding bookland.[5] One of the

1. Compare especially the editions of 1891 and 1903 in §§ 54 (p. 144) and 75 (p. 209).

2. See in the edition of 1903, the unfortunate use of the word *folkland* on pages 100, 118, 131, 138 and above all on page 202. This use is in contradiction with the previous explanation of the term in note 2 on p. 81. It is evident that Stubbs would have substituted *public land* for *folkland,* if these passages had not escaped him in his revision.

3. *Ibid.,* i, p. 83, note 2.

4. The old mistake about folkland is reproduced in Mr. Ballard's recent book, *Domesday Boroughs,* 1904, p. 124.

5. Edward, I, 2, in Liebermann, *Gesetze der Angelsachsen,* I, pp. 140–141.

two charters is a charter of exchange, granted by King
Ethelbert in 858; it is in Latin; in the text there is no
mention of folkland, but a note in Anglo-Saxon on the
back of the document indicates that the king has
converted into folkland a piece of land which he has
received in exchange for another.[1] The third document
is the will of the ealdorman Alfred, a document from the
last third of the ninth century; it deals with a piece of
land which is folkland and which the ealdorman wished
to pass on to his son (according to all appearances an
illegitimate son). He recognises that his son cannot enter
into possession of this land unless the king consents.[2]

In these three documents folkland is opposed, not to
private property, but to bookland, that is to say, land

"Folkland"
opposed to
"bookland"

held by charter. All sorts of difficulties
begin to appear if we understand by folkland the " land of the people," and, as
Mr. Vinogradoff has ingeniously shown, the scholars
who have followed Allen's interpretation have made
additions to it, in order to maintain it intact, by which
it has been rendered, really, more and more unacceptable. These difficulties vanish and the three texts
become as clear as possible if we return to the
explanation of the word folkland proposed in the
seventeenth century by Spelman. Folk-

and signifies
land held by
custom

land signifies not the land of the people,
public land, but the land held by popular
custom, by folk-right. Bookland is the
land held under franchises formally expressed in a
charter, a *book* : under the influence of the Church and
in consequence of the laws enacted by the king and the
witenagemot, this more recent kind of property escaped
old usages, and he who held it might dispose of it at
his will, whilst folkland, at least in principle, was
inalienable. It becomes clear to us that the law of

---

1. Kemble, *Codex diplomaticus aevi Saxonici*, ii, pp. 64—66, No. 281.
2. *Ibidem*, p. 120, No. 317.

Edward the Elder classifies every kind of property under the two rubrics of land held by custom and land held by a charter,[1] that King Ethelbert is converting a newly-acquired estate into folkland, inalienable property; that the consent of the king is necessary for the transmission to a bastard of folkland, a family estate subject to customary restrictions.

Thus folkland does not mean "public land." Stubbs gives his adhesion to this view a little unwillingly, it would seem,[2] in the passages he has carefully revised and corrected. But he maintains that there existed, at least until the end of the period of the Heptarchy,[3] a public land belonging to the people and distinct from the royal demesne. It was " the whole area, which was not at the original allotment assigned either to individuals or to communities. . . . It constituted the standing treasury of the country; no alienation of any part of it could be made without the consent of the national council. . . . Estates for life were created out of the public land . . . the beneficiary could express a

Stubbs maintains that there was a public land

1. The classification of the law of Edward, which recognises only folkland and bookland, *oththe on bóclande oththe on folclande*, would be incomplete and surprisingly erroneous, if folkland signified "land of the people." It would leave out of account family property transmitted hereditarily, as distinguished from holdings burdened with services; yet such property certainly existed then. It is doubtless this difficulty which has led certain defenders of Allen's thesis to suppose, without a shadow of proof, that the hereditary family estate had disappeared at an early date. There was another difficulty : this land, had existed in any case; was it not strange that no term denoting it specially was to be found in the Anglo-Saxon texts? This objection had already struck Kemble. As they did not realise that family landed property was called in Anglo-Saxon *folkland*, they sought for a name for it. Hence the terms *ethel* (invented by Kemble), *yrfeland* (invented by Pollock), to which Stubbs has made the mistake of giving currency. (See *Const. Hist.*, p. 81, note 2; compare, however, p. 80, note 1, restriction of the word *ethel*.) These appellations are not and cannot be founded on the authorities, for the good reason that the word denoting this kind of property was *folkland*.

2. In note 3 of vol. i, p. 81, Stubbs appears to hesitate and speaks of the "much contested term *folkland*."

3. "The public land," Stubbs supposes, "was becoming virtually king's land from the moment the West-Saxon monarch became sole ruler of the English." (*op. cit.* p. 212, cf. p. 100.)

wish concerning their destination in his will, but an express act of the king and the *witan* was necessary to give legal force to such a disposition. . . . The tribute derived from what remained of the public land and the revenue of the royal demesne sufficed for the greater part of the expenses of the royal house, etc." [1]

On what authorities is this theory founded? Stubbs, usually so precise, does not quote his authorities in his notes, speaks vaguely of " charters." It is easy to see that, whilst appearing to accept the interpretation of the word folkland which Mr. Vinogradoff rediscovered in Spelman, Stubbs retains a historical theory founded principally on the three texts of which we have just been speaking and on the erroneous explanation of the word folkland. His expression, quoted above, respecting the possessor of an estate in public land, who expresses a desire in his will with regard to the destination of that estate, is founded solely on the will of ealdorman Alfred; [2] now, as we have seen, Alfred expresses a wish relative to his *folkland,* which as a matter of fact is a family estate, and not a portion of *ager publicus.*

It has been claimed, it is true, that other documents in which the term folkland is not used, attest the existence of an Anglo-Saxon *ager publicus.* Mr.

Letter from Bede to Egbert Vinogradoff has clearly shown how unjustifiable such an interpretation is. The most celebrated of these documents is a letter of Bede to Egbert : the pseudo-monasteries of his time had caused so many estates, *tot loca,* to be given to them, that there did not remain enough to endow the sons of the nobles and warriors, *ut omnino desit locus ubi filii nobilium aut emeritorum militum possessionem accipere possint.* Stubbs concludes from this that " the sons of

---

1. See especially *Const. Hist.,* i, pp. 82–83, 202–203, 212. See also pp. 118, 127, note 4, 131, 138, 159, 302, etc.

2. It may be noted too that, in the document, there is mention of the consent of the king, but the *witan* are not referred to.

C

the nobles and the warriors who had earned their rest looked for at least a life estate out of the public land.[1] Who can fail to see that this translation of the words *loca, locus,* has arisen from a preconceived idea? It is perfectly allowable to suppose that the grants of which Bede speaks were made from the royal demesne. In England, as in France, men complained of the alienations from the royal demesne, or at least of the manner in which they were effected. That is all that Bede's letter proves.

It was doubtless with a view to restraining the imprudence of which Bede speaks that in the following century the witan intervened in matters of alienation of the demesne. The consent of the Witenagemot to alienations of land is an incontestable and interesting fact, but it has not the significance Stubbs attributes to

Consent of Witenagemot to alienations of land

it. We must begin by remarking with Mr. Maitland that this consent is at first very seldom expressed,—four times only in charters anterior to 750; it becomes habitual in the ninth century, then falls into desuetude, and from about 900 or 925 onwards is replaced by the mere mention of the confirmation by witnesses.[2] Again, there is no reason to attach a very special importance to the intervention of the witan in cases of alienation, since they dealt with all kinds of business; their very extensive political rôle is one of the characteristic features of Anglo-Saxon institutions. Finally, the mention we have of the consent of the witan in no wise confers more probability on the theory that there existed a public land distinct from the royal demesne. In the often quoted charter of 858 the land which Ethelbert alienates with the consent of his witan is called *terra juris mei.* We have no document in

1. *op. cit.* p. 171. The passage in Bede [ed. Plummer, i, 415] is quoted in note (2).

2. Cf. Stubbs, *Const. Hist.,* i, p. 212.

which the land the alienation of which the witan confirm or revoke appears as a part of the *ager publicus*.

Thus there is no ground for distinguishing between public land and royal demesne. The Anglo-Saxon kings had evidently in that respect ideas as vague and blurred in outline as our Merovingians, and it would be very singular if they had established a distinction between two things so difficult not to confound.

Stubbs' theory about Anglo-Saxon public land is therefore a weak part of his work. He was often enough unfortunate when he founded general theories on the work of others. But he was a scholar of incomparable perspicacity and sobriety when he studied the sources himself; this was most frequently the case, and it is for that reason that his book maintains its position.

———

III.

TWELFHYND-MAN AND TWYHYND-MAN.

A New Theory Respecting Family Solidarity among
the Anglo-Saxons.

According to the usual interpretation which has been
adopted by Stubbs,[1] the twelfhynd-man is the man who
Usual   has a wergild of 1,200 shillings, and the
interpretation   twyhynd-man is the simple ceorl, who has
a wergild of one-sixth of that amount. Similarly the
oath of the twelfhynd-man, in a court of justice, is worth
six times that of the ceorl. The intermediate class of
sixhynd-men possessed a wergild of 600 shillings.
Hynd, hynden is *hund*, a hundred. Twelfhynd-man
ought to be translated man of twelve hundreds, twyhynd-
man by man of two hundreds, etc.

In a fairly recent book, which is moreover a work of
absorbing interest, Mr. F. Seebohm proposes an entirely
                      different explanation, which serves him as
Interpretation   the foundation of his theory as to the
of Mr. Seebohm
                      importance of family solidarity in the
formation of Anglo-Saxon society.[2] According to him
the term *hynden,* which we find in the 54th chapter of
the laws of King Ini or Ine, has no numerical significance, and denotes the compurgators who support with
their oath a kinsman accused of murder. The
judicial oath of full value, which can aid a man most
effectively to purge himself of an accusation, is the oath
taken by the twelve oath-helpers of his kindred, having
each a complete family. In primitive times a great
number of relatives is an unquestionable advantage.

1. *Const. Hist.* i, pp. 128 note 4, 175, 178.
2. *Tribal Custom in Anglo-Saxon law,* 1902, pp. 406 sqq., 499 sqq.

The kindred aids the accused with the weight of its oath, or else by fighting for him when private war is inevitable, or else again by paying a share of his wergild. The *twelfhynd-man*, then, is the man in possession of a full kindred, which assures him the maximum of credit in the court of justice, and enables him to produce " twelve hyndens," that is to say, twelve kinsmen representing twelve groups ready to defend him. The *twyhynd-man* is the man who does not enjoy this advantage; he can only produce two oath-helpers, or at least those whom he produces are worth only " two hyndens," carry only one-sixth of the weight of the oath-helpers of the twelfhynd-man. Whether he be, by origin, an emancipated slave or a free man of low condition, or a native belonging to the conquered race, or an immigrant foreigner, he is in every case a man who has not a family sufficiently numerous to protect him when he is accused. The result for him is that he is obliged to seek the protection of a magnate, an act fraught with great consequences; the twyhynd-men thus form the class of tenants dependent on a lord, who at critical times takes the place, for his men, of the powerful kindred, which is at once the pride and the support of the twelfhynd-man.

The unfortunate thing is that Mr. Seebohm gives no convincing reasons for the new translation which he **Objections** gives of the *hynden* of Ini. There is no reason for rejecting in this passage its ordinary meaning : *hund,* a hundred.[1] Moreover, we

1. Chapter 54 of Ini (see Liebermann, *Gesetze,* i, pp. 112—115) is, moreover, very obscure. Mr. Chadwick in his *Studies on Anglo-Saxon Institutions* (1905), pp. 134—151 has minutely studied the question of the value of the oath expressed in hides. A relatively satisfactory interpretation of Chapter 54 can be deduced from his laborious researches, an interpretation which very nearly agrees with the translation proposed by Liebermann in his edition. The first clause of the chapter would signify : when a man is accused of murder and wishes to purge himself of the accusation by oath, it is necessary that for each hundred shillings (which the composition he is threatened with having to pay comprises) an oath should intervene " of the value of thirty hides." This oath of the value of thirty hides is that of the twelfhynd-man; it is worth six times that

have an authentic document on the scale of wergilds:
twelfhynd-man and *twyhynd-man* are explained in it in
the clearest manner; *hynd* and *hund* are brought together
in a manner which leaves no room for doubt.[1]

The traditional opinion implicitly accepted by Stubbs,
and adopted also in the most recent works [2] ought then
to be retained.[3] This remark does not, however, at all
diminish the importance which Mr. Seebohm so justly
attaches to the social results of family solidarity. The
participation of the kindred in the burdens and profits
of the wergild is a fact of considerable significance in the
history of law and manners, and the very terms whose
meaning we have just been discussing sufficiently prove
what a large share the wergild with all its consequences,
had in the formation of the Germanic communities.

of the twyhynd-man or simple ceorl. For example, if the composition to
be paid is 200 shillings, an oath proferred by two twelfhynd-men is
necessary. But Mr. Chadwick has not succeeded in explaining the origin
of the expression "oath of thirty hides." Mr. Seebohm, *op. cit.* pp.
379 sqq., quotes and comments on a passage from the *Dialogue of archbishop Egbert*, in which the hides are replaced by *tributarii*: a priest
swears "secundum numerum cxx tributariorum." Mr. Seebohm concludes
from this that the hide of the laws of Ini is "the fiscal unit, paying
gafol, which is designated by the *familia* of Bede." Mr. Hodgkin (in
the *Political History of England*, edited by W. Hunt and R. L. Poole,
i, 1906, p. 230) remarks that usually the ceorl did not possess five hides,
and that the thegns were far from all having the immense estates which
the different documents relative to the oaths seem to presuppose. According to him, the figures of hides given in these documents were entirely
conventional. On the meaning of *hyndena* and *hynden-man*, cf. Athelstan,
vi, 3, in Liebermann, *Gesetze*, i, p. 175.

1. "Twelfhyndes mannes wer is twelf hund scyllinga. Twyhyndes
mannes wer is twa hund scill'" (Liebermann, *Gesetze*, i, p. 392). That
is to say the wergild of a twelve-hundred-man is twelve hundred
shillings, the wergild of a two-hundred-man is two hundred shillings.

2. Besides Chadwick, op. cit., see P. Vinogradoff, *The Growth of the
Manor*, p. 125.

3. "The *six-hynd-man*," says Stubbs (*Const. Hist.*, i, p. 179, note 3)
"is a difficulty." Mr. Chadwick (op. cit., pp. 87 sqq.) proposes a fairly
satisfactory solution. The *sixhynd-man* would be sometimes a *gesithcund*
who can ride on horseback in the service of the king, without, however,
possessing the five hides necessary to be a *twelfhynd-man*,—sometimes
again a landowner having five hides, but of Welsh origin, and "worth" in
consequence only one half an English owner of five hides. This class of
sixhynd-men was doubtless hereditary and did not increase either from
above or below, since, at the end of the Anglo-Saxon period, there is no
longer any mention of it, and we must suppose it to have disappeared.
Cf. Seebohm, op. cit., pp. 396 sqq.

IV.

THE " BURH-GEAT-SETL."

STUBBS understands by the expression *burh-geat-setl* a right of jurisdiction without giving any further explanation.[1] It has been shown recently

The reading is incorrect

that the text to which he refers, the little treatise which he alludes to, following Thorpe, under the name of *Ranks,* and which is entitled in the *Quadripartitus :* " De veteri consuetudine promotionum," has been badly read. There should be a comma after *burh-geat* and *setl* should be taken with the words *on cynges healle* which come after.[2] It is thus that the phrase was understood in the old Latin translations. The compiler of the *Quadripartitus* says : " Et si villanus excrevisset, ut haberet plenarie quinque hidas terre sue proprie, ecclesiam et coquinam, timpanarium et *januam, sedem* et sundernotam in aula regis, deinceps erat taini lege dignus." The compiler of the *Instituta Cnuti* also writes : " . . . . et ecclesiam propriam et clocarium et coquinam et portam, sedem et privatum profectum in aula regis, etc." It is true that these Latin translations have not an indisputable

---

1. *Const. Hist.* i, pp. 86, 120, 210. H. Sweet, *Dictionary of Anglo-Saxon* (1897) says more explicitly : "Law-court held at city gate." Similarly Bosworth-Toller, *Anglo-Saxon Dictionary*: "a town gate-seat, where a court was held for trying causes of family and tenants, ad urbis portam sedes." As a matter of fact there is certainly no question of a tribunal held at the gates of a town. Mr. Maitland in *Domesday Book and Beyond* (p. 190 ; cf. p. 196, note 1) made a different mistake, and translated burh-geat-setl by "a house in the gate or street of the burh." 'Geat' cannot signify street. Mr. Maitland has given up this translation. See below.

2. The passage is as follows : "And gif ceorl getheah, thæt he hæfde fullice fif hida agenes landes, cirican and kycenan, bellhus and burhgeat, setl and sundernote on cynges healle. . . ." (Liebermann, *Gesetze,* i, pp. 456-457.)

authority. But Mr. Liebermann and before him Mr.
W. H. Stevenson[1] have pointed out that the palæo-
graphic mark of punctuation by which the word *geat*
is followed (a full stop having the value of a comma),
and the rhythm of the whole passage, equally forbid us
to take *setl* with *burh-geat*.

Setl, a very vague word, denotes in a general way a
Meaning of place; *geat* is the gate, and *burh* a
Burh-geat fortified place, town, or house. The
passage signifies therefore that, among the conditions necessary before a ceorl could become a thegn,
he must have an assigned place and a special office (*sundernote*) in the hall, the court of the king, and also a
belfry (*bell-hus*) and a " burh-gate." What does this
"burh-gate" mean ? Mr. W. H. Stevenson, the learned
editor of the *Crawford Charters* and of the *Annales* of
Asser, sees in it nothing but a rhetorical figure : the part
is taken for the whole, and the " burh-gate " means
simply the "burh," the fortified house. All idea of
jurisdiction ought therefore to be laid aside. Stubbs
and the other scholars who have made use of the passage
not only, in Mr. Stevenson's opinion, retained an un-
doubted misreading but interpreted the expression badly.
Mr. Maitland has rejected this last conclusion.[2] Mr.
Stevenson's article having been published in the most
widely-circulated English historical review, and Mr.
Maitland's refutation having possibly escaped the
notice of many readers, it seemed necessary to note here
that on the whole Stubbs was not mistaken as regards
the meaning of " burh-geat." Mr. Maitland points
out, in fact, the following clause in a charter granted to
Robert Fitz-Harding :[3] " Cum tol et them et zoch et
sache et belle et burgiet et infankenethef." The words

1. W. H. Stevenson, 'Burh-geat-setl,' in *English Historical Review*,
xii, 1897, pp. 489 sqq.

2. *Township and Borough*, 1898, Appendix, pp. 209-210.

3. Printed in John Smyth, *Lives of the Berkeleys*, i, p. 22 (quoted by
Maitland).

which surround " burgiet" here prove that there is
question of an " outward and visible sign of jurisdiction
or lordly power." The gate of the burh had become,
like the belfry, a symbol of the right of justice.
But for what reason? Miss Mary Bateson has quite
recently completed and simplified the explanation.[1]
She shows that the seignorial court was often held near
to the gate of the castle and to the belfry, and that a
natural relation thus established itself between the gate,
the belfry and jurisdictional power.

1. *Borough Customs*, ii, 1906, p. xvi, note 1.

V.

THE CEREMONY OF "DUBBING TO KNIGHTHOOD."

THE RECIPROCAL INFLUENCES OF THE ANGLO-SAXON AND FRANKISH CIVILIZATIONS.

STUBBS believes rightly that the practice of " dubbing to knighthood " was derived from a primitive and very
Origin of ceremony
widespread custom, and allows that an analogous usage may have existed among the Anglo-Saxons; but he is inclined to believe that they borrowed it from the Franks.[1] Recently the converse hypothesis has been put forth.

M. Guilhiermoz, in his fine *Essai sur l'origine de la Noblesse,* studies the history of dubbing.[2] He
Theory of M. Guilhiermoz
notices that the Germanic custom of the delivery of arms to the young man come to adult age, a custom described in the famous 13th chapter of the *De Moribus Germanorum,* is still to be distinguished, among the Ostrogoths, at the beginning of the sixth century; but afterwards it seems to disappear. Until the end of the eighth century the documents only speak of another ceremony, equally marking the majority of the young man, the *barbatoria,* the first cutting of the beard. From the end of the eighth century onwards, the ceremony of investiture reappears in the documents, while the *barbatoria* seems to fall into desuetude. Two explanations are possible; either the investiture took place, from the sixth to the

1. *Const. Hist.,* i, pp. 396-397, and note 1, p. 396.
2. *Essai sur l'origine de la Noblesse en France au Moyen Age* (1902), pp. 393 *sqq.;* see particularly p. 411, note 60.

eighth century, at the same time as the *barbatoria*, though it is not mentioned in the sources; that is the hypothesis which M. Guilhiermoz regards as most probable; or, on the other hand, " we might perhaps suppose that the solemn arming had disappeared among the Franks and that it only came into vogue again with them to replace the *barbatoria* as a practice borrowed from a Germanic people who had preserved it better . . . A passage in the life of St. Wilfrid of York, by Eddi, seems to allude to the custom of arming among the Anglo-Saxons at the end of the seventh century." [1]

Thus the Anglo-Saxons, who kept many Germanic institutions which the Franks had dropped, are supposed to have preserved the primitive usage described by Tacitus and to have transmitted it, towards the end of the eighth century, to Charlemagne and his subjects. The hypothesis is an interesting one, and connects itself with a class of considerations which Stubbs perhaps did wrong to neglect. As M. Guilhiermoz says, " a certain number of facts show the influence exercised in the Frank empire by Anglo-Saxon usages in the seventh and eighth centuries." The anointing of the kings in France, Brunner has noticed, was an Anglo-Saxon importation; so also was the custom of entrusting the young people brought up at the palace to the care of the queen.[2]

Influence of Anglo-Saxon civilization on the continent

The part that the scholars of the school of York played in the Carolingian Renaissance is well known. Carolingian painting, whose origins are complex and obscure, is beyond a doubt derived, in large part, from the early Anglo-Saxon art of miniature; and when we

---

1. " Principles quoque saeculares, viri nobiles, filios suos ad erudiendum sibi (to St. Wilfrid) dederunt, ut aut Deo servirent, si eligerent, aut adultos, si maluissent, regi *armatos* commendaret." M. Guilhiermoz takes this passage from Raine, *Historians of the Church of York*, i, p. 32.

2. Guilhiermoz, *loc. cit.* and pp. 92, 93.

compare the strange and striking productions of English painting in the tenth century with those of the Rheims school in the ninth, we may ask ourselves whether, far from having inspired Anglo-Saxon art a century after, the famous psalter of Hautvillers, or " Utrecht psalter," was not painted in France by Englishmen.

Stubbs has shown forcibly the influence of Carolingian institutions on English institutions.[1] It would be well, perhaps, to insist equally on the expansion of Anglo-Saxon civilization, which is in certain respects remarkable.

---

1. An influence which was only however very powerful in the 12th century. Stubbs describes this phenomenon of tardy imitation, with much learning, in his account of the reforms of Henry II (*Const. Hist.*, i, 656—7).

VI.

THE ORIGIN OF THE EXCHEQUER.

SEVERAL scholars, since Stubbs, have examined the perhaps insoluble question of the origin of the Exchequer, notably Mr. Round and quite

Recent work on the question recently Messrs. Hughes, Crump and Johnson.[1] These latter come to the conclusion that the financial organisation described in the celebrated treatise of Richard Fitz-Neal proceeded both from Anglo-Saxon and from Norman institutions. We should have in it therefore a typical example of that process of combination which formed the strength of the Norman monarchy, and which Stubbs has put in so clear a light. But in the searching study which he made of the Exchequer Stubbs refrained from distinguishing the elements of this institution with a precision that the sources did not appear to him to justify. Are there grounds for speaking with more assurance than he did? Let us see what we have learnt for certain which he has not told us.

The Exchequer, it will be remembered, comprised two Chambers, the *Inferius Scaccarium,* a Treasury, to which the sheriffs came to pay the *firma comitatus* and other revenues of the king, and the *Superius Scaccarium,* a Court of Accounts staffed by the great officers of the crown and personages having the confidence of the king, whose business it was to verify the accounts of the sheriffs on the "exchequer," and also to give judgment in certain suits. The thesis of Messrs. Hughes, Crump and Johnson is that the Treasury, the *firma comitatus* and the system of payment employed in the first years

1. In the introduction which they have prefixed to their critical edition of the *Dialogus de Scaccario* (1902), pp. 13—42.

after the Conquest, were of Anglo-Saxon origin, while the verification on the exchequer and the constitution of the staff of the Court of Accounts were of Norman origin. In short, an upper chamber of foreign origin was superimposed on a lower chamber already established before the Norman invasion.[1]

The Anglo-Saxon kings could not do without a Treasury. Stubbs admitted the existence of a " central department of finance" before the Conquest,[2]

Anglo-Saxon elements of the Exchequer

and the latest editors of the *Dialogus* will meet with no contradiction on that head. Let us add that we know even the name of the treasurer of Edward the Confessor. An inquest relative to the rights of the king over Winchester, made between 1103 and 1115, speaks of " Henricus, thesaurarius," who, in the time of Edward the Confessor, had a house in that town, at which the Norman kings themselves for a long time kept their treasure.[3] Two offices mentioned in the *Dialogus,* those of weigher (*miles argentarius*) and melter (*fusor*), appear to be anterior in origin to the constitution of the Exchequer properly so called, and evidently date, like that of the treasurer, from the Anglo-Saxon period.[4] Stubbs himself tells us that the *farm* paid by the sheriffs was tested by fire and weighed, and that this operation could not have a Norman origin. Thus the offices of treasurer, weigher, and melter, the *firma comitatus* and the method of verifying the value of the money date from the pre-Norman period. Mr. Round has pointed out

1. Hughes, Crump and Johnson, *op cit.*, pp. 14, 28.

2. *Const. Hist.*, i, p. 408, note 1.

3. Round, *The officers of Edward the Confessor*, in *English Histor. Review*, 1904, p. 92. Upon this inquest, see an article by the same author, in the *Victoria History of the Counties of England, Hampshire*, i, pp. 527 sqq.

4. In the time of Henry II, they were dependent on no other officer, and the author of the *Dialogus* was not sure whether he ought to connect them with the Lower Exchequer or the Upper Exchequer (*Dialogus*, i, 3; ed. Hughes, etc., p. 62). [Modern writers following Madox generally call the weigher pesour.]

that, contrary to an erroneous assertion of Stubbs, the " blanch-farm " is mentioned several times in *Domesday Book*.[1] Stubbs' proof might have been more complete and more exact, but on the whole his conclusion remains inexpugnable. No one is entitled to say, with Gneist and Brunner, that " the court of Exchequer was brought bodily over from Normandy." The pre-Norman origin of a part of the financial organisation of the twelfth century is a settled point.

Shall we now try to distinguish, with Messrs. Hughes, Crump and Johnson, the elements imported from abroad ? " The arithmetic of the Exchequer, like the main portion of the staff of the Upper Exchequer, is," they say, "clearly of foreign origin."[2] The 'clearness' they give us on that point is not dazzling. Let us see what it amounts to.

The "exchequer" was a cloth divided into squares by lines, with seven columns, each column including several squares; according to the place it occupied

Origin of the arithmetical system of the Exchequer at one or the other extremity a counter might signify one penny or 10,000 pounds.[3]

This arrangement suggested the idea of a game played between the treasurer and the sheriff,[4] and, according to Mr. Round, was intended to strike the eyes of the ignorant and to make the business easy to such unskilful accounters as were the sheriffs of the time of Henry I. It was out of the question to demand writings on parchment from them.[5]

The editors of the *Dialogus* think, on the contrary, that the system required " skilled calculators," and suppose

1. *The Origin of the Exchequer*, in : *The Commune of London and other Studies*, p. 66.

2. *Op. cit.*, p. 43.

3. See the description, *op. cit.*, p. 38 sqq.

4. " Inter duos principaliter conflictus est et pugna committitur, thesaurarium scilicet et vicecomitem qui assidet ad compotum, residentibus aliis tanquam judicibus ut videant et judicent." (*Dialogus*, i, 3 ; p. 61 of edition quoted.)

5. *Commune of London*, p. 75.

that the Anglo-Saxons were ignorant of it. Personally we share the opinion expressed by Mr. Round, and we find a difficulty in admitting that the English were not acquainted with the use of the abacus before the Norman Conquest. But let us approach the problem more directly. Can we determine the provenance of the arithmetical system described in the *Dialogus?* Stubbs notices that the term *Scaccarium* comes into use only in the reign of Henry I.,[1] and that until then the financial administration is called *Thesaurus* or *Fiscus*. Mr. Round quotes[2] a curious passage from the Cartulary of Abingdon, which records a lawsuit tried in the *Curia Regis* at Winchester, in the Treasury : " apud Wintoniam, in Thesauro;" we must perhaps conclude from this that at that moment, that is to say, in the first years of the reign of Henry I., the institution described later by the author of the *Dialogus* already existed in its essential features, with its attributes at once financial and judicial, but that the accounts of the sheriffs were not yet received on the chequered cloth, since the term *Scaccarium* has not yet replaced the term *Thesaurus*. Doubtless the sheriffs were accounted with by means of " tallies," the notched sticks of which Stubbs speaks. The author of the *Dialogus* tells us indeed : " Quod autem hodie dicitur ad scaccarium, olim dicebatur ad taleas." [3] It must then have been in the course of the reign of Henry I. that the substitution of the one system for the other was effected; henceforth the financial court called previously *Thesaurus* took, by extension, the name of *Scaccarium*, which denoted the table of account now in use, and which had been suggested by the appearance of the chequered cloth.[4]

1. *Const. Hist.*, i, p. 407.
2. *Commune of London*, p. 94.
3. *Dialogus*, i, 1 (Ed. Hughes, etc., p. 60).
4. "Licet autem tabula talis scaccarium dicatur, transumitur tamen hoc nomen, ut ipsa quoque curia, que consedente scaccario est, scaccarium dicatur. . . . Que est ratio huius nominis?—Nulla mihi verior ad presens occurrit quam quia scaccarii lusilis similem habet formam." (*Ibidem.*)

This is the very probable view accepted by Mr. Round. But we do not see that anyone is justified in concluding from it that " the arithmetic of the Exchequer is clearly of foreign origin." It would be necessary indeed to prove: (1) that this system of accounting was not known previously in England; we have already expressed our doubt on this head; (2) that it was employed previously on the Continent. The term Exchequer is only found in the countries occupied by the Normans, but it in no wise follows that it is of Norman origin. It may equally well be of English origin. The considerations brought forward on that point by Stubbs retain all their force, even since the discovery by Mr. Round in a Merton Cartulary of proof that there was an Exchequer in Normandy in 1130 at the very latest.[1] Indeed there is nothing to preclude the adoption of the chequered cloth in England being anterior by some years to this date.

The foreign origin of the Exchequer is not proved

No proof of a Norman origin of the Exchequer.

The Norman origin, therefore, of the arithmetic employed in the twelfth century is very far from being proved. As regards the staff of the Upper Exchequer, it is true that the great officers who sit there bear essentially French titles. When we compare the little work entitled *Constitutio Domus Regis* with the *Dialogus de Scaccario,* we note that " with a few exceptions every important officer in the financial department has his place in the household.

The staff of the Upper Exchequer may have been formed before the Conquest

---

1. *Bernard the King's scribe*, in *English Historical Review*, xiv, 1899, pp. 425 sqq. The document in question relates to a lawsuit regarding a Norman estate claimed by Serlo the Deaf from Bernard the Scribe. The suit was tried at the Exchequer : " Et ibi positus fuit Serlo in misericordia regis per judicium baronum de Scaccario, quia excoluerat terram illam super saisinam Bernardi, quam ante placitum istud disracionaverat per judicium episcopi Luxoviensis et Roberti de Haia et multorum ad Scaccarium, etc." The document as a whole shows that we have to do with a Norman Exchequer. The bishop of Lisieux, who presided over it, it seems, resided uninterruptedly in his diocese, and Robert de la Haie was seneschal of Normandy.

D

It may be added that the constitution of the household is so clearly of Frankish origin that it is not possible even to doubt that its organization was originally imported from abroad."[1]   But again, we must be agreed on the nature of the point at issue.   The important thing, be it remembered, is to distinguish what influence the Norman Conquest can have had on the development of the financial organization.

We have just seen that the method of verification of the accounts and even the name Exchequer may have arisen simultaneously in England and in Normandy or in England even earlier than in Normandy. As far as concerns the great officers sitting in the financial court, the Conquest of 1066 may have equally had no influence—for the good reason that these great officers existed in England before the Conquest of 1066, and that the court of Edward the Confessor was already profoundly "Normanised." Mr. Round, whom we have constantly to quote, has shown that this king had a marshal (named Alfred), a constable (Bondig), a seneschal (Eadnoth), a butler (Wigod), a chamberlain (Hugh), a treasurer (Henry), a chancellor (Regenbald), in short the same great officers who figured at the court of the Norman dukes.[2]   Did these personages take part in financial administration ?   It would be rash to affirm it at present.   But all that we know of the monarchical institutions of the West at that period equally forbids us to deny it.

To sum up, we see that some new documents have been contributed to the discussion, but without throwing any decisive light upon it.   The description **Conclusion** which Stubbs gave, thirty years ago, of the operations of the Exchequer, has been rectified and the details filled in, but his cautious conclusions upon the

1. Hughes, Crump and Johnson, Introduction, p. 14.

2. Round, *The officers of Edward the Confessor*, in *Engl. Hist. Review*, xix, 1904, pp. 90—92.

origin of the institution remain intact. He may have *Stubbs' conclusions* happened on other points to have underestimated *still hold.* excessively the effects of the Conquest of 1066 on the political development of England, but he appears to have been right in thinking that while the Exchequer manifestly contains certain Anglo-Saxon elements we cannot discern with certainty any element the introduction of which was the direct result of the Norman Conquest.[1]

1. See the bibliography of works relating to the Exchequer in Gross, *Sources*, § 50, and in the edition of the *Dialogus* referred to above, pp. vii—viii. The chief things to read are the article published by Mr. Round, in *The Commune of London and Other Studies*, and the introduction of Messrs. Hughes, Crump and Johnson, the merit of which we do not think of disputing. Mr. Round has brought to light the feudal, "tenurial" character of the two offices of Chamberlain and studied the mode of payment *ad scalam* and the *ad pensum* system; he has discovered also that the whole of the receipts and expenses did not appear in the Pipe Rolls, and that besides the Exchequer, the Treasury, which for a long time had its seat at Winchester, had its special accounts and its chequered cloth to verify them.

VII.

ENGLISH SOCIETY DURING THE FEUDAL PERIOD.

THE TENURIAL SYSTEM AND THE ORIGIN OF TENURE BY MILITARY SERVICE.

IN certain pages of his work Stubbs, either in dealing with the Norman Conquest or in order to give an understanding of the elements which composed the solemn assemblies of the *Curia Regis,* incidentally explains what an earl, a baron and a freeholder were, and expresses his opinion on the origin of tenure by knight-service.[1] We shall consider here the question as a whole, and at a slightly different angle, in order that the reader may the more clearly account for the differences which separate English and French society during that period.

(margin note) Differences from Continental Society

In spite of the " feudalization " of England by the Normans, the principles which distinguished men from one another in England were not the same as on the Continent. Differences of terminology already warn us that the institutions are not identical. The word *vassallus* is very seldom met with; *alodium*, in *Domesday Book*, does not denote an estate not held of a lord; but doubtless simply a piece of land transmissible to a man's heirs; it is very nearly the sense of *feodum*, which has a very vague meaning in English documents. It is said that So-and-so " tenet in feodo " if his rights are heritable, even when he has only the obligations of an agricultural tenant towards his lord.[2]

(handwritten margin note) alod = piece of land transmissible to a man's heirs.

1. *Const. Hist.,* i, pp. 283 sqq., 389 sqq., 604 sqq.
2. Maitland, *Domesday Book and Beyond*, pp. 152 sqq.; Pollock and Maitland, *History of English Law*, i, pp. 234 sqq., 297. It is to this last work that we chiefly refer the reader for all that follows. He will find there a notable exposition of what we call the "feudal institutions" of England. [On *feudum* and *alodium* in Domesday, cf. Vinogradoff, *English Society in the Eleventh Century*, pp. 232—8.]

And, indeed, there is, properly speaking, no distinct feudal law in England.   There, "feudal law is not a special law applicable only to one fairly definite set of relationships, or applicable only to one class or estate of men; it is just the common law of England." [1]   The English nobility is not therefore separated from the non-noble class, as in France, by a whole body of customs which constitutes for it a special private law.   It is public law which gives it a place apart and a superiority very different, for the rest, from those which the French baronage claimed.   The English baronage was founded by the Norman monarchy, and owed its riches and privileges to it.

No distinct feudal law

The *barones majores* are those whom the king has endowed with rich estates [2] and whom he summons to

---

1. Pollock and Maitland, *English Law*, i, pp. 235-236.

2. It is well-known that these estates, instead of forming compact principalities like those of the French dukes and counts, were generally scattered over several counties.   Mr. Round has proved that this disposition, a singularly favourable one to the monarchy and attributed by historians to the political genius of William the Conqueror, frequently originated in the uncompactness of the properties of the Anglo-Saxon thegns.   "It is often urged," he says, "that William deliberately scattered a fief over several counties in order to weaken its holder's power.   But this scattering might be only the result of granting the estate of a given thegn.   Thus, in Hampshire, Alured of Marlborough had, in both his manors, succeeded a certain Carle, who was also his 'antecessor' in Surrey and Somerset, and in the bulk of his Wiltshire lands.   Arnulf de Hesdin had for his predecessor, in his two Hampshire manors, an Edric, who was clearly also his 'predecessor' in the three he held in Somerset, and in some of his lands in Gloucestershire, Wilts. and Dorset.   In like manner Nigel the physician held lands in Wiltshire, Herefordshire and Shropshire, as well as in Hampshire, because in all four counties he had succeeded Spirtes, a rich and favoured English priest. On the other hand, a Domesday tenant-in-chief may have received a *congeries* of manors lying in a single shire.   Of this there is a very striking instance in the fief of Hugh de Port.   Except for two manors in Cambridgeshire, and one apiece in Bucks and Dorset, the whole fief lay in Hampshire," where he held fifty-six manors from the crown, and thirteen from the bishop of Bayeux.   (*Victoria History of Hampshire*, i, 421—422; cf. *Hertfordshire*, i, 1902, p. 277; cf. also the case quoted by F. M. Stenton, *Vict. Hist. of Derbyshire*, i, 1905, p. 305).

Mr. Round admits also that, side by side with the cases in which the companions of William received the entire estates of rich Englishmen, we have examples of Anglo-Saxon estates divided between several Normans, and estates formed for Normans from numerous small English estates. (*Vict. Hist. of Essex*, i, 353.)

The barons the *Commune Concilium* by individual letters; some of them are honoured by him with the title of earl and bear the sword of the earldom. The English aristocracy is to be a political aristocracy, a high nobility formed of privileged individuals, transmitting their power to the eldest son.[1]

In the same way the knights, who are to play so important a rôle in constitutional history, do not enjoy **The knights** a very peculiar personal status; but, as Stubbs shows, the carrying into effect of the judicial system inaugurated by Henry II. depends on their loyal co-operation; they are a class of notables, charged with judicial functions which can only be devolved upon men of trust. Apart from this distinctive feature, no barrier separates the knights from the rest of the freemen; military service is not strictly confined to the tenure by knight service, and the knight's fee might even be held by a freeman who was not a knight.

To sum up, in England there is no legal *personal* distinction except between the free and the un-free; but *liber* does not mean noble, although this **Meaning of** has been lately maintained.[2] In its *liber homo* narrower meaning, at least in certain passages, the *liber homo* of the English realm, far from designating the noble in opposition to the non-noble person, designates the non-noble freeman as opposed to the noble.[3] In its wider significance, *liber homo* means: one who is not a serf; it is in this sense that the Great Charter is granted to the *liberi homines* of the realm. It

1. On all this comments will be found, which if not original, are at least formulated with much precision and vigour, in E. Boutmy, *Développement de la Constitution et de la Société politique en Angleterre*, pp. 13 sqq., and English Translation by I. M. Eaden (*The English Constitution*), 1891, pp. 3 sqq.

2. According to M. Guilhiermoz, *Origines de la Noblesse*, p. 364, in England, *liberi homines* signifies *gentilshommes*, and *liberi tenentes* signifies possessors of noble fiefs or holdings. This theory is no truer of England than it is of France.

3. See the case of 1222 quoted by W. E. Rhodes, *Engl. Histor. Review*, xviii, 1903, p. 770: the rate of the contribution paid for the deliverance of the Holy Land is 1s. for the knight and 1d. only for the *liber homo*.

is as *liber homo,* not as noble, that the noble has personal rights.[1]

But social relations in England rested, above all, on another principle—that of *tenure,* which was applied to almost the whole of the population, from **Tenure** the king, from whom every tenure depends mediately or immediately, down to the humblest serf cultivating the land of his lord.[2] There was not an inch of English soil which was not subjected to this single formula : ' Z. tenet terram illam de . . . . domino rege,' Z. being either *tenens in capite* or separated from the king by more or less numerous intermediaries. This formula applies to all those who have a parcel of land, even to the farmer, even to the serf *cotter,* and it equally applies to the religious communities who hold land from a donor without owing him anything in return save prayers. Vagabonds and proletarians excepted, who must, I imagine, have existed always and everywhere in country and town,[3] all the English of the Middle Ages were tenants, and tenure, in the eyes of the lawyers, was much more important than personal status.[4] The distinction even between free and non-free in this country was practically a distinction between tenures much more than a distinction between persons.[5]

1. See the exposition and application of this fact in Pollock and Maitland, i, pp. 408 sqq.

2. See above, p. 23.

3. On the floating population of the country, the "undersette" and the "levingmen" see Vinogradoff, *Villainage,* pp. 213, 214.

4. Let us add that one and the same person might have tenements of different categories. Pollock and Maitland, *English Law,* i, p. 296, quote the instance of Robert d'Aguilon, who held lands from different lords, by military service, in sergeanty, in socage, etc.

5. See Pollock and Maitland, i, p. 232 sqq., 356 sqq., 407. The customs which we call feudal, such as rights of relief, of wardship, of marriage, etc., attached themselves not to the person but to the tenure by knight service. In practice, of course, they were subjects of the keenest interest for members of the nobility, and it is for this reason, that, in the Great Charter, the baronage took particular precautions to prevent the crown from abusing them. Pollock and Maitland, pp. 307 sqq. study these customs and try to determine in what measure they were peculiar to the tenure by knight service. Sometimes tenure in socage was subject to the rights of wardship and of marriage.

Let us leave aside servile tenures, of which we have spoken in studying the problem of the manor. The free tenures at the end of the historical period dealt with in Stubbs' first volume may be grouped into the following principal types :—

Free tenures

1. Tenure in *frankalmoin, in liberam elemosinam*, in free alms. It is theoretically the land given to the Church, without any temporal service being demanded in return ; it is agreed or understood that the community will pray for the donor. In practice, tenure in frankalmoin admits of certain temporal services, and its clearest characteristic, at the end of the twelfth century, is that judicially it is subject only to the ecclesiastical forum.

Tenure in frankalmoin

2. Tenure by knight service, *per servitium militare.* The holder of a knight's fee owes in theory military service for forty days. In the twelfth century the king often demanded, instead of personal service, a tax called scutage.[1] The usual rate was two marks on the knight's fee, and it has been pointed out that that sum was equal to the

Tenure by knight service

1. Stubbs discusses scutage in several passages ; see vol. i, pp. 491-492, 494, 624-625. He rightly remarks that this term did not always denote a tax to replace military service. But, both in regard to the origin of scutage and in regard to the obligations imposed, when it was levied, on those who held land by knight service, he should have taken account of recent work, and not have contented himself with referring in a single line to Mr. Round's article which is in absolute contradiction with some of the conclusions to which Stubbs continued to adhere. Mr. Round took up the question of scutage again, in the course of a bitter controversy with Mr. Hubert Hall, editor of the *Red Book of the Exchequer* (See the bibliography in Gross, No. 1917). An excellent piece of work by an American scholar, J. F. Baldwin, should also be read : *The scutage and knight service in England*, Chicago, 1897. Briefly, there is no ground for considering scutage as an innovation of the reign of Henry II ; the tax in substitution for military service and even the word *scutagium* already existed under Henry I. On the other hand, scutage only dispensed from military service if the king thought fit : his subjects had not the right to choose (See Pollock and Maitland, *English Law*, i, pp. 267 sqq.) Scutage, from the beginning of the 13th century, came to be a tax like any other ; no exemption was granted in exchange. Mr. Baldwin shows, moreover, that its financial importance has been exaggerated. The question of scutage will be definitely elucidated when all the Pipe Rolls anterior to the middle of the 13th century, the period at which scutage fell into desuetude, have been published and studied.

pay of a knight hired for forty days. The king's servants reckoned, in the thirteenth century, that William the Conqueror had created 32,000 knights' fees. It has been calculated that in reality the king of England could not count on more than 5,000 knights.[1] Legally, military service was a *regale servitum*. The right of private war was not recognised. In practice, the lords reckoned on the knights whom they had enfeoffed to sustain their personal quarrels and not merely to provide the service demanded by the king from each of his tenants-in-chief; there were some even who maintained more knights than their obligations towards the king required.

3. Tenure in serjeanty. The *servientes,* serjeants (officers of every kind from the seneschal or the constable **Tenure in serjeanty** to the cook or messenger), received land from the king or the lord whom they served on a tenure called *serjanteria*. The obligations of this tenure were sometimes agricultural, sometimes military. Holders of military serjeanties only differed from knights by their lighter equipment.

4. Tenure in free socage, *in socagio*. From the end of the twelfth century it can be said that all free tenure **Tenure in socage** which is neither frankalmoin nor knight service nor serjeanty, is tenure in socage. Land can be held in socage by the most diverse persons; by a younger son of a family, who has received it from his father, by a great personage who holds it of the king on condition of a rent or of agricultural services, or, finally, a very ordinary case, by free peasants. These last owe the lord a rent or services, and their economic condition frequently approaches that of the un-free villeins; but these freeholders are bound directly to the king by an oath of allegiance, often take even an actual oath of homage to their lord and form part of the county court and the juries.

1. Round, *Feudal England*, pp. 264—265, 292.

In the category of tenure in socage we may class the tenure in burgage, peculiar to the burgesses of the towns with charters.

Tenure in burgage

What is the origin of the English tenures? The systematization, the symmetrical simplification and the legal theory of tenure are due to the Norman lawyers; this is not disputed. The difficulty, as we have already seen in studying the evolution of the agricultural classes, is to ascertain in what proportions the feudal and seignorial principles brought from the Continent by the Norman invaders underwent admixture with Anglo-Saxon traditions in order to produce, in the world of reality, the new régime. Stubbs approached the problem from several sides, but never stated it with all the clearness desirable. We have already said that several scholars of our generation, notably Messrs. Maitland and Round, have done much to define its terms and advance its solution, although they are far from being always in agreement.

Origin of English tenures

We have treated of the origin of peasant tenures above. There is another side to the problem, if not as interesting at least as obscure : this is the origin of feudal military service and of tenure by knight service. Mr. Round seems to have definitively elucidated this difficult subject. It is another reason for giving it our attention for some moments; Stubbs was content to refer, in a note, to Mr. Round's article, without modifying, as he should have done, the rather confused and hesitating pages which he devotes to the knight's fee and knight service.

Problem of military service and of tenure by knight service

Stubbs, and with him the historians of the Germanist school, such as Gneist, Freeman, and, in our own day, Mr. Maitland, have more or less a tendency to see in the military organization of the last Anglo-Saxon centuries "a strong impulse towards a national feudalism." [1]

Germanist theory. Anglo-Saxon origin

1. *Const. Hist.*, i, p. 208.

The king's warrior is the thegn, that is to say, according
to Stubbs, the man who possesses five hides of land of
his own;[1] moreover, we see that in Berkshire, in the
reign of Edward the Confessor, it was the custom to
furnish a warrior (*miles*) for every five hides. Military
service is not yet attached to a special tenure, but the
military obligation is linked already with the possession
of land instead of being, as formerly, a personal
obligation of the whole free population. Stubbs thinks
that, England once subjected by the Normans, " the
obligation of national defence was incumbent as of old
on all landowners, and the customary
service of one fully-armed man for each five
hides was probably the rate at which the
newly-endowed follower of the king would be expected
to discharge his duty." [2]

Unit of service in the host

According to Gneist, William the Conqueror made
this Anglo-Saxon usage into a legal rule which he
imposed " on the entire body of old and new possessors
of the land; " but the rate of five hides was only an
approximate indication, and in reality military obligations were fixed according to the productive value of the
estates (Gneist even thinks that the principal object of
Domesday Book was to permit of this fixing of military
obligations). The *feuda militum*, the knights' fees, were
units worth £20 a year.

Stubbs takes the same view, adding that nevertheless

1. Stubbs, adopting the views of K. Maurer, claims (i, p. 173) that
the name of *thegn* was given to all those who possessed the proper
quantity of land, that is to say five hides. This theory is inadmissible.
It is founded on two wrongly interpreted texts. One of them is that
which we have quoted above in our note on the *Burh-geat*, p. 39 note 2.
We need only read it as a whole to perceive that more than the possession
of five hides was required in order to become a thegn. The holding of
five hides was doubtless the normal and traditional estate of the thegn,
but there were *rustici* who possessed as much or more land, without
thereby becoming thegns. See A. G. Little, *Gesiths and Thegns*, in
English Histor. Review, iv, 1889, pp. 726—729.
2. *Const. Hist.*, i, pp. 284 sqq. We are trying here to give a coherent
account of the thesis of the Germanists, and we shall not bring out the
contradictions in detail which Stubbs' argument presents; Mr. Round
does this (*op. cit.*, pp. 232-233).

Stubbs holds that the Normans adopted the established Anglo-Saxon rule of military service for 5 hides of land.

Gneist holds that William I made the unit of military service land worth £20 a year.

Some thing more than the possession of 5 hides necessary to constitute a thegn.

" it must not be assumed that the establishment of the knight's fee was other than gradual."

Gradual formation of the system

William the Conqueror did not create the knights' fees at a stroke; there is, as regards this, a great difference between the state of things which is described in *Domesday* and that which the charter of Henry I. allows us to divine, and we may even say that the formation of the military fiefs took more than a century to accomplish, and was not yet completed in the reign of Henry II. It was the subject of a long series of arrangements.[1]

Thus Anglo-Norman military tenure would be derived from the Anglo-Saxon usages, and nevertheless would only have been established very slowly.

Mr. Round's objections.

Mr. Round[2] has no difficulty in showing the weakness of these theories. If the number of knights which each great vassal had to furnish to the king depended on the number of hides in his estates or on their value in annual revenue, if the king required a knight for each unit of five hides, or for a land unit producing £20 a year, and if the knight's fee represented that unit precisely, what remained for the baron? Obliged to divide the whole of his estate into military fiefs, was he then despoiled of all? The supposition is absurd; the argument of Stubbs and Gneist, however, leads directly to it. Moreover, the alleged slowness with which the feudal military system constituted itself is not seriously proved. The argument *ex silentio* drawn from *Domesday Book* is worth nothing, first, because the object of Domesday was fiscal not military, and, secondly, because a closer study of that document demonstrates beyond question the existence of military tenure. We are told that under the first Norman kings certain great estates were not yet divided into knights' fees; but we must not conclude from this that they were

1. *Const. Hist.*, i, pp. 285 sqq., 468 sqq.
2. *Introduction of knight service into England* in *Feudal England*, pp. 225 sqq.; cf. his *Geoffrey de Mandeville*, p. 103, and *Vict. Hist. Worc.* i, 250.

not subject to military obligations; here lies the chief flaw in Stubbs' argument. On his reasoning it would seem that the existence of feudal military service and the existence of knights' fees were bound up together, and that the king had himself to devise a rule for the formation of these fees. But this was not the case. In order to form his host, the king addressed himself to his barons,[1] his tenants-in-chief alone, and demanded from each of them so many knights; but the manner in which each of them procured them did not concern him directly.

Gneist, Stubbs and Freeman, Mr. Round very rightly remarks, lose sight of the real problem to be solved, and immerse themselves in generalisations and vague writing about the " gradual evolution " of the institution. " For them," he writes,[2] " the introduction of knight-service means the process of sub-infeudation on the several fiefs; for me it means the grant of fiefs to be held from the crown by knight-service. Thus the process which absorbs the attention of the school whose views I am opposing is for me a matter of mere secondary importance. The whole question turns upon the point whether or not the tenants-in-chief received their fiefs to hold of the crown by a quota of military service, or not. If they did, it would depend simply on their individual inclinations, whether, or how far, they had recourse to sub-infeudation. It was not a matter of principle at all; it was, as Dr. Stubbs himself puts it, " a matter of convenience," a mere detail. What we have to consider is not the relation between the tenant-in-chief and his under-tenants, but that between the king and his tenants-in-chief: for this was the primary relation that determined all below it."

1. I use "baron" here in the sense which it generally has of direct vassal, tenant-in-chief. Mr. Tait (*Mediæval Manchester*, 1904, pp. 14 sqq·, 182 sqq.) observes that in the 11th and early part of the 12th century any considerable military tenant might be called a baron whether he held of the crown or not. Little by little the appellation was restricted to the tenants-in-chief.

2. *Feudal England*, p. 247.

Mr. Round next asks himself what were the obligations imposed by William upon his tenants-in-chief; he concludes that the Conqueror, without issuing any written grants or charters, nevertheless fixed the obligations of each great vassal and himself settled the *servitium debitum*.[1]

It was William the Conqueror who established feudal service

Examining, elsewhere, the replies given by the barons in 1166 to the inquest ordered by Henry II.,[2] he remarks that, save for rare exceptions which cannot invalidate the principle, the barons and the bishops owe to the king a number of knights varying from 10 to 100,[3] and which is always a multiple of 10 or of 5. If the assessment of the *servitium debitum* conformed to a precise estimate of the value of the barony, the adoption of these round figures is incomprehensible; we can understand it on the contrary, if we observe that the English *consta-*

The amount fixed in relation to the unit of the host

This shown by the number of Knights required being always a round figure.

1. Mr. Round chiefly invokes the testimony of the monastic chroniclers. He quotes in addition the following unpublished writ, which he dates 1072 : " W. rex Anglorum, Athew' abbati de Evesham salutem. Precipio tibi quod submoneas omnes illos qui sub ballia et justitia sunt, quatinus omnes milites quo[s] mihi debent paratos habeant ante me ad octavas Pentecostes apud Clarendunam. Tu etiam illo die ad me venias et illos quinque milites quos de abbatia tua mihi debes tecum paratos adducas. Teste Eudone dapifero. Apud Wintoniam." (*Feudal England*, p. 304.)

2. The object of the inquest of 1166 was to fix and as far as possible increase the resources which might be expected from scutage, which was paid, as is well known, on the *scutum* or knight's fee. Mr. Round has shown very well how the replies of the barons were always interpreted to their disadvantage. These *cartae* of the barons, transcribed in the *Black Book* and the *Red Book* of the Exchequer, answered the following questions : How many knights had been provided with a knight's fee in the barony before the death of king Henry I? How many since? If the number of knights' fees created was not equal to the number of knights to be furnished, how many knights *on the demesne*, that is to say, not enfeoffed, did the baron furnish? What were the names of the knights? Apropos of the expression *super dominium*, Mr. Round (p. 246, note 57) points out one of the "marvellously rare" lapses, which can be found in Stubbs; the latter has wrongly interpreted (see *Const. Hist.*, i, p. 285, note 3) the reply of the bishop of Durham. This prelate, as a matter of fact, declared that he had already created more than 70 knights' fees. Upon the tenures of the bishopric of Durham, see an article by G. T. Lapsley, on the *Boldon Book*, in *Victoria History of the County of Durham*, i, 1905, pp. 309 sqq.

3. Robert son of Henry I. alone furnished 100 knights. It is even rare for the *servitium debitum* to reach 60 knights : the most frequent figures are 30 and under.

bularia consisted of ten knights, and that the Normans,
were already, at the time of the Conquest, acquainted with
the military unit of ten knights. It was natural that the
demands of the king from his barons should be based,
not with exactitude on their resources, which, moreover, it
was impossible for him to know with complete precision,
but on the necessities and customs of the military system.
"As against the theory that the military obligation of
the Anglo-Norman tenant-in-chief was determined by
the assessment of his holding, whether in hidage or in
value, I maintain that the extent of that obligation was
not determined by his holding, but was fixed in relation
to, and expressed in terms of, the *constabularia* of ten
knights, the unit of the feudal host. And I, consequently, hold that his military service was in no way
derived or developed from that of the Anglo-Saxons,
but was arbitrarily fixed by the king, from whom he
received his fief." We believe, with Mr. Round, that
this solution is correct, and that it "removes all
difficulties."

To go back to the question which has drawn us into
following Mr. Round in his long discussion, we see
Origin of the two series of military holdings that the origin of military tenure or
tenure by knight service is a double one:
the barony was as a general rule a military
holding conferred by the king from the first days of the
Conquest, in return for the service of so many knights;
the lands enfeoffed by the barons to knights in order to
be able to fulfil the said obligation towards the king
constituted a second series of military holdings.[1]

This second series was formed slowly, gradually, as
Stubbs says, and the crown only began to concern itself
directly with them and claim to regulate the number of
these sub-tenancies after the lapse of a century, at
the time of the inquest of 1166, at a moment when the

1. Mr. Round, pp. 293 sqq., admits that the knight's fee was normally
an estate yielding an annual revenue of 20 pounds.

tax for the redemption of service, the *scutage* of one or two marks on the knight's fee attracted the attention of the financiers of the exchequer. It seems as if the inquest of 1166 might have given military tenure a precision and stability which it had not as yet; but the fiscal aims which the officials of the Exchequer pursued were very soon to take from tenure by knight service its primitive reason for existence and its true character. In the thirteenth century military tenure will be simply the tenure which involves payment of scutage; thus it began to decline from the time it was regularised, a fairly frequent phenomenon in the history of institutions.

What view are we to take now as regards the links some have sought to discover between the Norman military tenure and the service of the **Mr. Maitland's theory respecting Anglo-Saxon military service** Anglo-Saxon thegn? Mr. Round rejects every idea of filiation, and even declares that his theory on the introduction of knight service into England opens the way to the examination, on a fresh basis, of kindred problems, which should be viewed from the feudal point of view, and not with the set purpose of seeing Anglo-Saxon influences everywhere. Mr. Maitland, who has since published his *Domesday Book and Beyond,* and the second edition of his *History of English Law,* admits, as proved in the " convincing papers " of Mr. Round, that the number of knights furnished by each barony was actually fixed by William the Conqueror. But he questions whether the Normans really thus introduced into England a principle which was not already applied there. Even the notion of a contract between him who receives a piece of land and him who gives it in return for military service was not foreign to the English. The ecclesiastical administrators who granted land to thegns were not squandering the fortune of the saints for nothing : they evidently intended to provide themselves with the warriors whom

Maitland shews that the elements of feudalism already existed in England.

their land owed to the king. Such a state of things might adapt itself to a feudal explanation; perhaps even it might give rise to it. We do not know what system was practised in the east of Saxon England, where the seignorial power was weak; but in the west the substance even of the knight's fee already existed. The Bishop of Worcester held 300 hides over which he had *sac and soc;* he had to furnish 60 *milites*; now at the beginning of the reign of Henry II., it is the same number of 60 knights which is imposed upon him.[1]

We find it difficult and even somewhat futile to choose between the view of Mr. Round and that of Mr. Maitland.

No direct influence upon Anglo-Norman service in the host

It is probable that the Normans, at the moment of the Conquest, were entirely ignorant of the very complex and varied institutions of the Anglo-Saxons, and that, if they had found nothing in England analogous to the feudal system, they would none the less have imposed their feudal ideas and customs, conquerors as they were, and but little capable, moreover, of rapidly grasping new social and political forms. On this ground, and if we ask ourselves for what reasons William the Conqueror brought over into England the system of service in the host as it existed in France, Mr. Round may quite legitimately deny all filiation between tenure by knight-service and the five hides of the thegn about which, doubtless, the Conqueror did not trouble himself.[2]

But England was prepared by her past to receive and develop the feudal organisation on her soil. She was

1. *Domesday Book and Beyond,* pp. 156 sqq.; see also pp. 294, 307–309, 317. Pollock and Maitland, *History of English Law,* i, pp. 258-259.

2. King's thegns still exist in the reign of William the Conqueror. But they do not rank with the tenants-in-chief by military service. In Domesday they are placed after the serjeants of the shire. As a distinct social class, they disappear during the reigns of the Conqueror's sons. (See the article by F. M. Stenton on the *Domesday* of the county of Derby in *Vict. History of Derbyshire,* i, 1905, p. 307).

E

acquainted with commendation, with land held from a lord or from several lords superimposed,

The feudal régime finds a favourable soil for original development

with military service due to a lord; under the form of the heriot, she was acquainted even with the right of relief; seignorial justice was widely established.[1] England, therefore, easily accepted the seignorial and feudal régime; but of necessity she impressed her stamp upon it. Anglo-Norman society in the twelfth century differed from French society in very important points. Words and things show this clearly; tenure in socage, which little by little absorbed all the free tenures of the Middle Ages and still exists to-day, is an Anglo-Saxon term and is derived from the status of the *sochemanni*. It has been said that the Anglo-Saxon régime had only produced dismemberment and anarchy, and that the Norman Conquest arrested this disintegration by the introduction of the feudal system; but did not this dismemberment and this anarchy proclaim the spontaneous formation of a native feudal system? What the Norman Conquest brought to England, which England had not at all, either in reality or germ, was not feudalism, it was a monarchic despotism based on administrative centralisation.

1. Mr. Round in the studies which the editors of the *Victoria History* are publishing, insists on the divergences between the Norman feudal system and Anglo-Saxon institutions (*Victoria History of Surrey*, i, 1902, p. 288, *Hertfordshire*, i, 1902, p. 278; *Buckinghamshire*, i, 1905, p. 218). Mr. Maitland, however, does not pretend to deny these divergences.

VIII.

THE ORIGIN OF THE TOWNS IN ENGLAND.

THERE exists no satisfactory general account of the origin of the towns in England.[1] The pages devoted to this question by Stubbs, in three of the chapters of Vol. I.,[2] have long been the safest guide to consult. But during the last fifteen years this problem has been the subject of studies based on thorough research which have advanced its solution, and even those with which Stubbs was able to make himself acquainted and which he has quoted sometimes in the notes to his later editions might have been turned to greater profit by him. The researches of Mr. Gross, the ingenious and disputable theories of Mr. Maitland, the discoveries of Mr. Round and Miss Mary Bateson, notably, deserve to be known by our readers. With their help we must now draw out a summary sketch, in which we shall make it our chief endeavour to give the history of the English towns its proper place in the framework of the general history of the towns of the west.

France in the Middle Ages was acquainted with infinitely varied forms of free or privileged towns, and very diverse too are the names which were used to designate them from North to South. In England the degrees of urban enfranchise-

Novelty of the question (marginal note)

The "borough" (marginal note)

---

1. For the bibliography, see Ch. Gross, *Bibliography of British Municipal History*, 1897. It is an excellent repertory. But since 1897, some very important works have appeared, notably those of Miss Mary Bateson. Some years ago, English municipal history was backward compared with that of France; but the activity now displayed in that respect by scholars on the other side of the Channel contrasts with the present scarcity of good monographs on the French towns.

2. *Const. Hist.*, i, pp. 99—102, 438—462, and 667—676.

ment are less numerous,—the upper degrees are wanting—and, in addition, a somewhat peculiar term is applied to the privileged town in the later centuries of the Middle Ages : in opposition to the *villa*, to the *township,* it is called *burgus, borough,* and the municipal charters often contain in their first line the characteristic formula : " Quod sit liber burgus." [1] Hence in the works of English scholars who concern themselves with the origin of municipal liberties, the word borough is constantly made use of. It seems to us, necessary, however, to get rid of this word, which uselessly complicates and confuses the problem to be solved, and it is well to give our reasons at the outset.

The term "borough" is confusing.

The first idea that the word *borough* summons up is that of the " bonne ville " as it used to be called in France; that is to say, the town which sent representatives to the assemblies of the three estates. In fact, in the fourteenth and fifteenth centuries, the borough is the town which is represented in the House of Commons. But if we are not content to stop short at this external characteristic, and if we enquire in virtue of what principles a town is selected to be represented in Parliament, we are obliged to recognise that such principles do not exist, that the list of boroughs is arbitrarily drawn up by the sheriffs, and that it even varies to a certain extent. In the period before the application of the parliamentary system, is the boundary line which separates the boroughs from the simple market towns and villages any clearer?

The difficulty of defining the borough

The parliamentary criterion

Already, in his valuable book on the gild merchant, which is so full of ideas, facts and documents, Mr. Gross had observed that the term *liber burgus* is a very vague one, applying to a group of franchises the number of which gradually grew in the course of centuries, and

---

1. See, for example, in Stubbs' *Select Charters,* 8th edition, pp. 311, 313, etc. Upon this expression see below, page 69, note 2.

none of which, if we examine carefully the relative position of the *burgi* and the *villae*, was rigorously reserved to the *burgi*, or indispensable to constitute a *burgus*.[1]   First among them was judicial independence :
The judicial criterion   the burgesses of the *liber burgus*[2] had not to appear before the courts of the shire and the hundred.[3]

In a quite recent work Miss Mary Bateson expresses the opinion that we have there in fact the characteristic of the borough : it is by its court of justice that the *borough*, detached from the hundred and forming as it were a hundred by itself, is distinguished from the Norman period onwards, from the township and the market town.   It may have been originally a township, it may continue to be a manor in the eyes of its lord; it is none the less, from a legal point of view, an entirely special institution, which has its place outside the shire and the hundred.   It is not a slow evolution, it is a formal act, which gives it this place apart, and which makes of the word borough a technical term corresponding to a definite legal conception.[4]   Undoubtedly there is much

[Margin note: Mary Bateson holds that a borough is distinguished by having its own court of justice]

1. Gross, *Gild Merchant*, 1890, i, pp. 5 sqq.   Cf. A. Ballard, *English boroughs in the reign of John*, in *English Histor. Review*, xiv, 1899, p. 104.
2. According to Mr. Tait (*Mediæval Manchester*, p. 62; Cf. Pollock and Maitland, *History of English Law*, i, 639) the expression *liber burgus* would denote simply the substitution of the tenure in *burgagium* and its customs for the villein services and *merchetum* of the rural manor; and where it does not appear in the charter, it is because burgage-tenure existed before the granting of the charter.   We do not think that this interpretation is sufficiently broad.   *Liber burgus* often has a much more general sense, notably in the following document of the year 1200 relating to the town of Ipswich (published in Gross, *Gild Merchant*, ii, p. 117 : " Item eodem die ordinatum est per commune concilium dicte villate quod de cetero sint in burgo predicto duodecim capitales portmenni jurati, *sicut in aliis liberis burgis Anglie* sunt, et quod habeant plenam potestatem pro se et tota villata ad gubernandum et manutenendum predictum burgum et omnes libertates ejusdem burgi, etc."
3. Upon the great importance of the jurisdiction of the English towns in the early period, a jurisdiction which extended to "causae majores," see Mary Bateson, *Borough Customs*, ii, 1906, p. xx.
4. Mary Bateson, *Mediæval England*, 1903, pp. 124, 125; cf. the same author's, *Borough Customs*, i, 1904, pp. xii sqq.; controversy with Mr. Ballard in *English Historical Review*, xx, 1905, pp. 146 sqq.

truth in this theory. But we cannot decidedly accept it
in its entirety. The court of justice did not suffice, any
more than the tenure in *burgagium* or the *firma burgi,*
to constitute a *borough,* at the period at which men
claimed to distinguish clearly between the *boroughs* and
the market towns.[1] And, *a fortiori,* this must have
been the case during the Norman period.

The criterion of "incorporation" We might be tempted to admit, with Mr.
Maitland, that it is the character of a
corporation,[2] which is the essential part in the conception
of a *borough.* But " incorporation " is a legal notion,
for which the facts no doubt prepared the way, but
which was not stated in precise form until towards the
end of the thirteenth century. For the twelfth and
preceding centuries we must give up the attempt to find
an exact definition of *burgus.* During the Anglo-Saxon
period, and even in the eleventh century, the word *burh*
had an extremely general signification. It does not even
exclusively denote a town, but is also applied to a
fortified house, a manor, a farm surrounded by walls.[3]

It should be observed that the important towns are
also designated, for example in *Domesday Book,* by
the name of *civitates;* like almost all the words in the
language of the Middle Ages, *civitas* and *burgus* have
no precise and strict application.[4] The difficulty would
be the same, or nearly so, if one attempted to define the
French *commune* not in an *a priori* fashion but after
comparison of all the passages in which the word is

1. See the case of Manchester : Tait, op. cit. pp. 52 sqq. Cf. Pollock
and Maitland, *English Law,* i, 640.

2. *Corpus corporatum et politicum, communitas,* etc. See Gross,
Gild Merchant, i, pp. 93 sqq.; Pollock and Maitland, i, pp. 669 sqq.;
and above all Maitland, *Towship and Borough,* 1898.

3. W. H. Stevenson, in *English Historical Review,* xii, 1897, p. 491.

4. In France, *civitas* denotes a bishop's see; and this is often the case in
England, but not uniformly. Cf. Maitland, *Domesday Book and
Beyond,* 1897, p. 183, note 1; *Township and Borough,* p. 91; Round, in
Victoria History of the counties, Essex, i, 1903, pp. 414, 415. Upon the
definition of the modern city, see G. W. Wilton, *The county of the city*
in the *Juridical Review* (Edinburgh), April, 1906, pp. 65 sqq.

employed. In the same way that there is an advantage in making use of this convenient word to denote our most independent towns, it may be of service to use the word *borough*, when we are studying the **Necessity of laying aside this term** English towns of the end of the Middle Ages. But, for the period of origins, which is the only one we have before us at present, it is better not to embarrass ourselves with this expression which by its misleading technical appearance has perhaps greatly contributed to plunge certain English scholars into blind alleys. It will be enough to ask ourselves how the towns were formed which have a court of justice and a market, which have a trading burgess population, which have sooner or later obtained a royal or baronial charter, and which, both by a variable body of privileges and by their economic development, have distinguished themselves from the simple agricultural groups; whether they were destined to be called boroughs or market towns matters little.

There is no imperious necessity for formulating the problem any differently from the way it has been formulated for the towns of the Continent, and it is for this reason that we have not entitled this essay : *The Origin of the Boroughs.* The question which directly interests general history is to know how the English towns were formed. It is doubtful whether this problem can ever be solved with absolute certainty,[1] but that is no reason for not approaching it at all.[2]

---

1. Cf. the reflections of Mrs. Green, *Town Life in the fifteenth century*, 1894, Preface, p. xi. Mrs. Green appears to think that it is better to lay aside for the present the study of municipal origins.

2. We make no pretence of treating here of the problem of the origin of municipal liberties, or of explaining what those liberties were. Stubbs has dealt very fully with the question, and we should risk repeating him. A systematic enumeration of the privileges of the "boroughs" will be found in Pollock and Maitland, *English Law*, i, pp. 643 sqq., and the excellent book of Ch. Gross, *The Gild Merchant*, may be read with the greatest profit; the second volume of this work is composed of original documents of the highest interest for English municipal history as a whole.

Domesday Book alone can give a solid point of departure for this study. The relatively abundant

The sources sources of the Anglo-Saxon period, laws, charters or chronicles, furnish only a very meagre quota to what we know of the towns before the Conquest. It is fortunate again that the " tempus regis Edwardi " was a matter of interest to the commissioners of King William, that we can project the light emanating from *Domesday* on the later times of Anglo-Saxon rule,—obscured though that light may often be.[1]

The most serious gap in our sources may be guessed: we have no information as to the filiation which may

The question of Roman origin exist between certain English towns of the Middle Ages, and the towns founded on the same site by the Roman conquerors.[2]

During the period of the Roman domination there were no great towns in England.[3] It is believed that

Roman towns in England Verulamium (St. Albans, in Hertfordshire) was a *municipium;* only four *coloniae* are known : Colchester, Lincoln, Gloucester and York. London was already the principal commercial centre, but we know almost nothing about it. There was without doubt a fairly large number of little towns; the names of some thirty of them have come down to us. Winchester, Canterbury, Rochester, Dorchester, Exeter, Leicester, etc., existed, and doubtless had a germ of municipal organisation. But, in the first place, we know nothing of this organisation, no important municipal

1. On the mainly fiscal nature of Domesday, in which, moreover, a certain number of very important towns do not figure, see Maitland, *Domesday Book and Beyond*, pp. 1 sqq., and A. Ballard, *Domesday Boroughs*, 1904, pp. 1 sqq.; above p. 18.

2. We have still less information, naturally, respecting Celtic origins. London seems to have arisen from a small, pre-Roman town. It is well known that the first mention of London is to be found in the *Annales* of Tacitus, bk. xiv, c. 33, ad ann. 61 : "Londinium . . . . copia negotiatorum et commeatuum maxime celebre. . . ."

3. See the works cited above, p. 12, note 3. On the places at which the Romans built towns see Haverfield, *Romano-British Warwickshire*, in *Victoria History of Warwickshire*, i, 1904, p. 228.

inscription having been preserved. Again, we have no idea what became of the Romano-British towns during the tempest of the invasions. At least the precise knowledge which we possess only relates to the disappearance of certain of them, burnt by the Anglo-Saxons, or else completely abandoned, like that curious

Silchester Calleva Attrebatum (near the present village of Silchester, in Hampshire), of which it has become possible to say—so much have excavations been facilitated in our day by this rapid and definitive abandonment—that it is the best known archæologically of all the Roman provincial towns. Calleva Attrebatum, after the extinction of the imperial government (about 407), was still inhabited for about a century; a recent discovery has shown that they had again begun to speak and write the Celtic language there; then, at the approach of the Germanic invaders the town was completely evacuated, and has never since been inhabited.[1] Other towns, such as Winchester (Venta Belgarum), appear, on the contrary, to have survived the catastrophes of the sixth century; but we know nothing of their ancient institutions.[2] It is more than probable that they resembled those of the Roman towns of the

Romanist theories Continent, and in consequence differed essentially from the municipal franchises of the Middle Ages. Nevertheless Th. Wright[3] and H. C. Coote[4] have asserted the continuity of municipal life in England, the filiation of the urban institutions of

1. See the very interesting articles by Mr. Haverfield : *The last days of Silchester*, in *English Histor. Review*, xix, 1904, pp. 625 sqq.; *Silchester* in the *Vict. Hist. of Hampshire*, i, pp. 271 sqq. Cf. *ibidem*, pp. 350 sqq., the archæological description by G. E. Fox and W. H. St. John Hope. See also the description of Castor, near Peterborough, in *Victoria History of Northamptonshire*, i, 1902, pp. 166 sqq. Mr. Haverfield believes that Castor was an old Celtic settlement.

2. See Haverfield, *Victoria History of Hampshire*, i, pp. 285 sqq.

3. *The Celt, the Roman and the Saxon, illustrated by ancient remains*, 1st edition, 1852, 4th edition, 1885.

4. *A neglected fact in English History*, 1864; *The Romans of Britain*, 1878.

the Middle Ages and of the Roman period. We can only repeat what Stubbs says of this same theory which he found again in Pearson's *History of England*. All the analogies on which the Romanists rely are susceptible of a different and much more probable explanation.[1] He might have added that most French scholars agree to-day in rejecting this filiation as far as concerns even the most profoundly and anciently Romanised parts of Gaul where municipal life was most intense.[2] What chance remains of there having been continuity in a country like Great Britain in which the imperial domination was much less solidly established? The humble village, with its tenacious agricultural customs, was able to maintain itself as it was, so it is supposed, in the storm of the Germanic conquest, but not the municipality with its institutions.

Certain towns, however, in the material sense of the word, were able, I repeat, to survive the great catastrophe. In spite of the disdain of the Germans for

Probable persistance of some settlements

fortified refuges, the ramparts of the Roman towns and imperial fortresses must have been utilised, doubtless even kept in repair for a certain time by the invaders as well as by the invaded,[3] and certain Anglo-Saxon *burhs* must have been only the continuation or the resurrection of Roman fortified places. Such may have been the case with Winchester, Lincoln, Canterbury. In Gaul, a great number of Roman towns perished during the invasion; others, in spite of terrible misfortunes continued to be inhabited, while losing every vestige of their ancient political institutions; life concentrated itself in some particularly favourable quarter, easy of defence, or, with the materials of the abandoned houses, a square *castrum*

1. *Const. Hist.*, i, p. 99, note 3.

2. See Flach, *Orig. de l'ancienne France*, ii, pp. 227 sqq.

3. One of the most ancient Anglo-Saxon charters, No. 1 of the *Codex Diplomaticus* of Kemble, dated 604, speaks of a rampart (wealles).

was constructed, to which the sadly reduced population confined itself.[1] It is probable that this phenomenon of the preservation of fragments of urban life occurred in Britain as elsewhere, and the Germanists have no serious grounds for denying its possibility. In the material sense of the word, certain English urban groups may have continued the Roman town.

Stubbs, we have seen, does not put this supposition absolutely aside. For the rest, if his study of the Anglo-Saxon town is a little wanting in clearness and vigour, at any rate it avoids thereby the faults of too systematic an exposition, and when he examines the formation of the *burh,* which, in his eyes, is nothing but " a more strictly organised form of the township," [2] he assigns a great share to the most diverse influences, and the wealth and variety of the information which his text and notes furnish has not perhaps been sufficiently noticed or turned to profit. We believe with him that in England, as in France, many of the urban communities grew out of pre-existent villages.[3] The rural, agricultural character of the town is particularly remarkable in England during the whole of the Middle Ages. Those who study its history, " have fields and pastures on their hands." [4] Part of the townsmen—doubtless the descendants of the most ancient inhabitants—are

Formation of English towns. Different influences

Towns born from villages

1. See Flach, *op. cit.*, pp. 238–9; Pirenne, *Orig. des constitutions urbaines*, in *Rev. Historique*, lvii, pp. 59 sqq.

2. We may guess what reading and comparisons inspired Stubbs with this theory, which derives the institutions of the town from those of the village, and which is rejected to-day by most scholars, doubtless in too absolute a manner : G. L. von Maurer, whose ideas had so much influence on him, alleges in his *Geschichte der Städteverfassung in Deutschland* (1869—1871) that every town is derived from a mark community. Since then, von Below has adopted the theory again in a less inadmissible form (*Ursprung der deutschen Stadtverfassung*, 1892) ; cf. Vinogradoff, *Growth of the Manor*, p. 148.

3. See the case of Derby in F. M. Stenton's article on the Domesday of Derbyshire, *Victoria History of Derbyshire*, i, 1905, pp. 308, 309.

4. Maitland, *Township and Borough*, p. 9.

husbandmen, the cultivated lands are sometimes found even inside the walls, and whatever may have been said to the contrary there are lands belonging to the community of burgesses.[1]

But the towns must have developed above all " in the places pointed out by nature as suited for trade," [2] whether these places were still uninhabited or whether ancient Roman towns or villages existed there already. It was the interest of the kings and magnates to create markets there, which brought them in good revenues, and to guarantee the security of trade; [3] merchants perhaps founded colonies there, as in Germany and France. The "great monasteries in which the Anglo-Saxon bishops had their sees," were also by their economic importance, by the industrial and commercial needs, which the service of religion gave rise to, by the attraction which celebrated relics exercised, centres of urban concentration and work, and Stubbs notes that in the Anglo-Saxon version of Bede the equivalent given for *urbana loca* is *mynster-stowe*.[4]

Influence of commerce

The monasteries

Throughout the West the castles also formed the nuclei of urban groupings; they offered a refuge in case of attack, and it was the lord's interest to have for his neighbours artisans and

Military origins

1. Cf. Maitland, *op. cit.* and *Domesday Book and Beyond*, pp. 200 sqq.; J. Tait, *English Historical Review*, xii., 1897, p. 776; and Ballard, *Domesday Boroughs*, pp. 87 sqq.

2. Stubbs, *Const. Hist.* i, 99.

3. On the creation of markets, the prohibition of buying and selling elsewhere, the idea of preventing the sale of stolen objects, the market peace, etc., see Maitland, *Domesday Book and Beyond*, pp. 192 sqq.

4. The inventory of the rents and dues owing to the Abbey of St. Riquier (Hariulf, *Chron. de Saint Riquier*, ed. Ferd. Lot, 1894, Appendix vii) shows us, as early as the year 831, a numerous population of lay artisans grouped in streets according to their trades around that abbey, and in return for lands which are granted to them, furnishing some, tools, others bindings, or clothes or articles of food, etc. This very curious document has, it seems to us, the value of a general explanation, in the history of the monasteries and the monastic towns of the West.

merchants who could supply him with cheap goods.[1]
It must have been the same in England. In any case
it is quite clear that at one period every English town
took on a military character. We may assume that this
transformation which was to complete the constitution
of towns clearly distinct from villages, took place in the
time of Alfred. Until then the word *burh* denoted not
a town, but a fortified house belonging to a king or a
magnate.[2] In the eighth century the urban settlements,
old or new, with the exception perhaps of those which
may have grown up around one of these fortified houses,
no longer had or never had any serious defence; so that
the Danes, when they invaded eastern England in the
ninth century, occupied the towns without resistance.
By constructing military works for their own use they
completed the lesson they were giving the English.

[marginal note: The towns before Alfred were not fortified.]

---

1. The formation of the town of Bruges is quite characteristic. It
was, doubtless, the favourable geographical situation of the castle of the
count, which caused the town to become a great commercial city instead
of remaining an insignificant market town like so many of those which
arose around castles (Cf. Pirenne, *op. cit., Revue Historique*, lvii,
p. 65.) But there are many favourable sites to be met with where no
town has ever been founded. It was the castle of Bruges which, to all
appearance, determined the formation of the town; see the very typical
passage from Jean le Long reproduced in Fagniez, *Docum. relat. à
l'Hist. de l'industrie et du commerce en France*, 1898, i, No. 95 : " Post
hoc ad opus seu necessitates illorum de castello ceperunt ante portam
ad pontem castelli confluere mercemanni, id est cariorum rerum merca-
tores, deinde tabernarii, deinde hospitarii pro victu et hospicio eorum
qui negocia coram principe, qui ibidem sepe erat, prosequebantur, domus
construere et hospicia preparare, ubi se recipiebant illi qui non poterant
intra castellum hospitari ; et erat verbum eorum : "Vadamus ad pontem" :
ubi tantum accreverunt habitaciones, ut statim fieret villa magna, que
adhuc in vulgari suo nomen pontis habet, nempe *Brugghe* in eorum
vulgari pontem sonat." True—and M. Fagniez should have pointed this
out to his readers—Jean le Long flourished in the fourteenth century;
and, as Dom Brial observes (*Historiens de France*, xviii, p. 593), he is
not always able to distinguish the false from the true in the sources he
consults. But there is every reason to accept his account of the con-
struction of the castle of Bruges by Baldwin ' Bras de fer,' count of
Flanders, in the time of Charles the Bald, and consequently the tradition
which he recounts concerning the foundation of the town deserves
attention.

2. On the ancient significance of the word *burh* and the *burh-bryce*,
see Maitland, *Domesday Book*, p. 183. On the manner in which the
burhs were fortified, see Round, *The Castles of the Norman Conquest*,
in *Archaeologia*, lviii, 1903.

alfred built fortifications to resist the blancs

Alfred (871—900) knew how to profit by it and created fortified places; and it is from his time that the word *burh*, instead of only denoting fortified houses, is also employed in the sense of town. We see in the Anglo-Saxon chronicle that the valiant warriors, the *burh-ware*, of Chichester and of London, contributed greatly to the success of the war against the Danes. Edward the Elder, son of Alfred (900—924) continued to found *burhs*.[1] We understand henceforth why the documents tell us of *cnihts* dwelling in the towns, and why the first city gilds are *cnihtengilds*.

Mr. Maitland has thrown a flood of light upon this foundation of military towns, which occupy a special place in the county, bear the same name

The county towns

as the county throughout the greater part of England,[2] and in some cases are planted at its geographical centre. The strategic value of these new towns explains why some of them are so small; it is not commercial prosperity nor density of population that gives the latter the special institutions which distinguish them from villages which are sometimes much larger; it is the fact that they are fortified places.

Maitland's theory that towns were garrisons, established by the lord or the county to fulfill their obligation

Mr. Maitland goes further. He seeks to explain by purely military causes the differentiation which took place between the township and what he

The "garrison theory"

calls the borough; on a study of *Domesday Book* which is certainly ingenious and suggestive, he bases a hypothesis which has been called the " garrison theory;" and he has been followed by another scholar, Mr. Ballard, who systematizes and exaggerates his theory.

1. In 923, Manchester was fortified and occupied by a garrison, and this is the first mention which we have of that town (Tait, *Mediæval Manchester*, pp. 1 sqq.).

2. The counties lying to the North of the Thames nearly all bear the name of their county-towns; for example Oxford-shire (see list of counties in Stubbs, i, p. 107). Upon this question, see Ballard, *Domesday Boroughs*, pp. 4 sqq.

Certain towns described in *Domesday Book*, these two scholars observe, are characterised by tenurial hetero-

The passages on which it is founded

geneity, being composed of houses which belong, some (the majority) to the king, others to this or that Norman lord, lay or ecclesiastic; and these houses before the Conquest belonged, some to the king, others to some thegn or other. Thus at Oxford the *burgenses* and their houses or *haws* appertain in some cases to the king, in others to a prelate (the Archbishop of Canterbury, the Bishops of Winchester, of Lincoln, of Hereford, of Bayeux, of Coutances, the Abbot of Abingdon, etc.), in others again to a Norman lord (the Count of Mortain, the Count of Evreux, Walter Giffard, etc.). *Domesday* affords evidence that this is not a Norman innovation, for it gives us a list of *thegns* of the county of Oxford who, before the Conquest, so held houses in the " borough " of Wallingford. Moreover, the possession of many of these houses was in direct relation with the possession of such and such a manor in the rural part of the county; indeed the *Domesday* compiler frequently mentions the manor instead of the lord, and indicates how many houses the manor has in the borough : for example, the manor of Doddington has five *haws* in Canterbury. It is specified that before the Conquest, " tempore regis Edwardi," there were in Canterbury 259 houses thus attached to manors; and the rural estates possessing houses in Canterbury numbered thirteen. Not only houses but burgesses appertained to manors : eighty burgesses of Dunwich appertain to one of the manors of Ely, twenty-four burgesses of Leicester to the manor of Ansty, etc. These statements which puzzle the reader of *Domesday,* become intelligible and coherent, if we suppose that every town characterised by tenurial heterogeneity dated from the period at which the Danish invasion had to be repelled, that it was originally essentially a military post, and that its garrison and the upkeep of its ramparts were the concern of the whole county. We can understand then why, side by side with ordinary houses, there are houses which are appurtenances of rural estates, and why, at

Mural houses Oxford, these houses bear the name of *mansiones murales,* and are burdened with the special charge of maintaining the fortifications of the town.[1] Freemen are in fact subject to the *trinoda necessitas,* the triple duty of repairing bridges, serving in war, and maintaining fortifications; the great rural proprietors who wish to acquit themselves of this last obligation without displacing their men, have a house in the town, furnished with *burgenses,* who when the king gives the order, will put in a state of defence the part of the ramparts the care of which is their charge. Many of the *burgenses,* moreover, are warriors, *cnihts,* and are maintained by the king and the great proprietors of the surrounding countryside : in this way is to be explained the mention in *Domesday* of *burgenses* attached to such and such a rural manor. In short, the primitive "borough" is essentially a fortress kept in a state of defence by the inhabitants of the county.

Later, at the end of the Anglo-Saxon period, the military spirit in the borough became enfeebled, a fact which explains the relative ease of the

Decay of the system. The homogeneous boroughs Norman Conquest and the difficulty which we have in reconstituting the real character of the earliest towns. In addition there grew up on the royal demesne, or upon the estates of powerful men, urban groups which obtained tardily, perhaps subsequently to the Conquest, the privileges which the simple townships did not enjoy. These are the homogeneous 'boroughs,' which are dependent on a single lord; for example, Steyning, which belongs to the Abbot of Fécamp, and whose

1. The service of *burh-bot* and the custom of Oxford are noted by Stubbs, *op. cit.* i, p. 102, note 4.

burgesses are all the Abbot of Fécamp's men. But the real 'borough,' the primitive *burgus*, is that which, at the date of *Domesday Book*, is still dependent on numerous lords.[1]

This theory is confronted unfortunately by unsur- *This theory un-* mountable objections.[2] If the inhabitants of a county *tenable.*

Objections ought to " contribute " to the upkeep of the ramparts and of the garrison of a particular " borough," and if it is thus that we must explain the mention of houses and burgesses appurtenant to rural manors, how comes it that *Domesday Book* speaks of houses appurtenant to manors which are not situated in the same county as the "borough " in which these houses stand? Why is it impossible to establish a proportion between the number of burgesses furnished by a manor and the extent of that manor, and how is the fact to be explained that a single manor of the Church of Ely maintains eighty burgesses at Dunwich?[3] Why are there so many manors exempt from the burden of maintenance, why are there only three which have duties towards the town of Chester? Moreover, the peculiarities of *Domesday Book,* which

1. Mr. Maitland (*Domesday Book and Beyond*, pp. 176 sqq.) only considers specially characteristic the boroughs described in Domesday at the beginning of their county, apart from the general arrangement of fiefs, and so to speak in direct relation with the county itself. It is these that he calls *county towns,* and Mr. Ballard (*Domesday Boroughs,* p. 5) calls *county boroughs.* But according to Mr. Ballard (p. 43) there are other "boroughs " (he gives them the queer name of *quasi county boroughs*) which are not separately described at the beginning of the county, and which yet ought, from the point of view which he is taking, to be classed with the first category ; the difference which separates them is of a fiscal nature, and does not directly concern the " garrison theory."

2. See the reviews of *Domesday Book and Beyond* by J. Tait, and of Ballard's work by Miss Mary Bateson, in the *English Historical Review,* xii, 1897, pp. 772 sqq. and xx, 1905, pp. 144 sqq. Cf. Round, in *Victoria History of Surrey,* i, 1902, pp. 285-286 ; *Hertfordshire,* i, 1902, p. 295 ; *Essex,* i, 1903, p. 385 ; *Berkshire,* i, 1906, pp. 310 sqq. Mr. Round more particularly corrects the mistakes of Mr. Ballard.

3. Dunwich, moreover, is simply described as a manor, *manerium,* in *Domesday Book.* But Mr. Ballard inserts in his list of "boroughs," all the localities to which *Domesday Book* attributes *burgenses,* and applies the garrison-theory to all of them.

F

the garrison theory claims to render intelligible, are for the most part capable of a simpler interpretation. Miss Bateson has elucidated the position of the *burgenses* appurtenant to rural manors in a very satisfactory manner. They were evidently non-resident burgesses, country people, who, with a view to gain, bought the freedom of a town, in which they might do a profitable trade. The eighty *burgenses* of Dunwich, appurtenant to a manor of the abbey of Ely, had doubtless bought their title, in order to come and buy the herrings which the monks needed, in that port. The houses appertaining to rural lords might serve as occasional lodgings, storehouses, etc. . . . We may add that comparative history does not allow us to consider the " tenurial heterogeneity " of so many English towns very surprising. Material and political dismemberment is the dominant feature of the French and German towns up to the eleventh century. The town was nothing but a juxtaposition of patchwork, of fragments of great estates.[1] There is no reason for attributing an absolutely original growth to the English towns, and it is, in our view, singularly rash to spin theories on their origin without constantly recalling to mind the conditions under which the towns of the Continent appear to have developed.

We propose then to accept the views of Mr. Maitland on the foundation of numerous fortified places in the time of Alfred and his successors, but to **Early importance of commerce** reject his theory, made even less acceptable as systematized by Mr. Ballard, on the alleged distinction, of a purely military character, between the " borough " and the township. The creative element of this distinction was doubtless, in England as on the Continent, commerce. Even at the period of the creation of the military *burhs* the economic factor must

1. Flach, *Orig. de l'ancienne France*, ii, pp. 243 sqq ; Pirenne, in *Revue Historique*, lvii, pp. 62 sqq.

[Margin note: The so-called "garrisons" were really non-residents, established in the town for purposes of trade. — Bateson.]

have played its part; except in some cases in which strategic considerations stood in the way, the king doubtless chose trading places, which it was all important to defend and convert into defensive centres, for fortification and the development in them of the military spirit: such was evidently the case with London. It is evident, besides, that the transformation of a town into a *burh* must have singularly facilitated the development of its trade, since the king's peace specially protected *burhs*. A good situation on a navigable river or on an old Roman road, and commercial traditions, on the one hand, the special security due to the ramparts, the garrison, the king's peace, on the other hand, may have thus had a reciprocal action. The military occupation of the towns thus completed and did nothing but complete the work accomplished under the powerful stimulus of commercial and industrial needs. And it is significant that, in the Anglo-Saxon laws, we sometimes find the town designated by the name of *port*,[1] and that numerous charters tell us of a town's officer called port-reeve or port-gerefa.[2] The *port* is the place of commerce; it is the old name for a town in Flanders, where civic origins have a clearly economic character.[3]

Reciprocal Influences

The "port"

Thus the Anglo-Saxon towns, like the towns of the

1. Notably in a passage in the laws of Athelstan, in which *port* is clearly synonymous with *burh* (Liebermann, *Gesetze*, i, pp. 155—159, §§ 14 and 14, 2).

2. Stubbs, *op. cit.* i, 100, 439, 440, 451, note 2. There is also the *port-moot* or *port-man-moot*, the *port-men*, etc. These words apply to inland towns as well as to sea-ports.

3. The different causes which favoured the growth of towns can be clearly distinguished in the county of Durham. According to the *Boldon-Book*, this county possessed five towns at the end of the 12th century. The external conditions which had determined their development were: at Durham, the castle and the church; at Norham, the castle; at Wearmouth, the sea-port; at Darlington, the high-road; at Gateshead, the close vicinity, on the other bank of the Tyne, of the town of Newcastle, of which Gateshead was in some sort the suburb. See the article by Lapsley on the *Boldon-Book*, in *Victoria History of Durham*, i, pp. 306 sqq.

Continent, were formed in the places in which the insufficiency of agricultural life made itself felt, where the chance of leading a less laborious, more spacious, even safer life than that of the peasant offered itself. In England, as elsewhere, the monastery and the castle served as nuclei of urban concentration. There as elsewhere the creation of markets attracted colonies of traders, and, thanks to the special protection of the king, the town was an abode of peace, a peace safeguarded by a doubtless rigorous penal code. There as elsewhere walls gave the citizens a security unknown to the rustic population. The Anglo-Saxon town, it is true, possesses a special franchise : it is a hundred by itself, it has its *moot,* its court of justice. It owes this point of superiority over the French town to the survival of the Germanic institution of the hundred among the Anglo-Saxons. But, like the towns of the Continent at the same period, it is heterogeneous, split up, and its judicial unity is interfered with by private jurisdictions; *sac* and *soc* correspond to immunity.[1] It has no corporate unity : it has indeed associations, gilds; but these are pious or charitable brotherhoods, clubs whose main business is to brew beer and drink it at the common expense;[2] they are not corporations taking part in the government of the town. Of merchant gilds, whose

Features of resemblance to the continental towns

1. Whilst attaching due importance to the interesting popular institution of the *moot,* we should remember that in the continental towns, justice had not entirely fallen into private hands, and that the cases of the merchants escaped the immunists. Already, in the Carolingian empire merchants were protected by the public authority, and it followed that disputes in matters of weights and measures and business transactions continued to belong to the public jurisdiction. Many merchants, moreover, were subject to no private jurisdiction, from any point of view. See Pirenne, *op. cit., Revue histor.,* lvii, pp. 78 sqq., and pp. 86 sqq., for the importance of the *jus mercatorum,* [of which a useful account is given in Mitchell's *Law Merchant* (1904).] Upon this last point, cf. L. Vanderkindere, *La première phase de l'évolution constitutionelle des communes flamandes,* in *Annales de l'Est et du Nord,* année 1905, pp. 365 sqq.

2. See the article by J. H. Round on the inquest of Winchester, in *Victoria History of Hampshire,* i, p. 532.

interest it would be to manage common affairs, there is as yet no trace either in the documents of the Anglo-Saxon period or even in *Domesday;* it has been proved, moreover, that later, when there were merchant gilds, they did not constitute the kernel of municipal adminis-tration. And this is another feature common to the towns of England and those of the Continent, that the gild, while it was an element of progress and of joint defence against oppression, was not the creative element of civic self-government.[1]

From what Stubbs says it is evident that we are as badly informed respecting the inner life of the primitive

Urban institutions English towns as respecting that of the towns of the Continent.[2] We know nothing which allows us to assert the existence of a true municipal patriciate; there is no proof that the possessors of sac and soc, such as the *lagemen* of Lincoln, had administrative powers. We see clearly what the burdens weighing upon the 'burgenses' are : payment of *geld* and dues in kind (*firma unius noctis* and others) to the king, payment of *gafol* to the lord of the manor, military service, etc.; but we do not see what their liberties are. It is true that the description of such liberties was not one of the objects for which the Anglo-Saxon charters and *Domesday Book* were drawn up. It is very probable, moreover, that, as early as the eleventh century, the burgesses, emboldened by wealth and peace, had sought for safe-guards against the financial tyranny of the royal officers, had dreamed of independence; they had evidently more cohesion and strength than the inhabitants of the country. They asked to be allowed to pay the sheriff an annual fixed sum, instead of numerous little imposts which made exactions easy; at Northampton the *firma*

1. See Gross, *Gild Merchant*, i, pp. 77 sqq.; Hegel, *Staedte und Gilden* (1891).

2. Stubbs, *Const. Hist.*, i, p. 100 sqq.

burgi already exists at the time of *Domesday*. At this period, the movement of revolt against seignorial oppression has already begun in some continental towns. Everywhere the increase of moveable wealth created a powerful class of townsmen, careful to safeguard their material interests and able to enforce their claims.

It would perhaps be allowable to say that from that time forward divergencies show themselves between the towns of England and those of the rest the

Continental influences after the Conquest West. And yet, while it is true that city-republics analogous to those of Italy or Flanders are not found across the Channel, we must not think that the island was not open to continental influences. The present generation of English scholars has only quite recently set itself to determine these influences, and the results obtained have already changed all received ideas as to the development of the English towns. " Our characteristic belief that every sort of ' liberty ' was born of ideas inherently English," writes one of these scholars,[1] " must receive another check, and must once more be modified to meet certain facts that have failed to obtain due recognition."

Mr. Round has shown that the maritime towns forming the confederation of the Cinque Ports had, with **The Cinque Ports** their mayor and their council of twelve *jurats,* a constitution of French origin, that they were acquainted with the essentially Flemish and Picard penalty of demolition of the offender's house,[2] and he thinks that the very idea of this confederation—

[margin note: The liberties of the towns not wholly worked out in England.]

1. Miss Mary Bateson, *The Laws of Breteuil,* in *English Histor. Review,* xv, 1900, p. 73.

2. Mr. Round is wrong, however, in saying that this punishment existed in England only in the Cinque Ports. I find it in the Customs of Preston : "Pretor de curia colliget firmam domini regis ad quatuor terminos anni, et ibit semel propter firmam, et alia vice, si placuerit ei, *deponet hostium cujuslibet burgensis, etc.*" (*Engl. Histor. Review,* xv, 1900, p. 497). Other instances have been quoted by Miss Bateson in her *Borough Customs,* i, pp. 30, 264, 280 and ii, pp. 38—40.

analogous to certain French collective communes and christened, moreover, by the French name of " Cinque Ports,"—was borrowed from Picardy.[1]

We shall summarize and discuss further on Mr. Round's articles on the history of London ; according to that scholar we have there an example of communal revolution analogous to those of France and suggested by them.   Finally, a more certain fact, the Norman

---

1. *Feudal England,* pp. 552 sqq. Professor Burrows, in his *Cinque Ports* (Historic Towns), held that this privileged confederation was in existence before the Norman conquest. Mr. Round, *op. cit.,* vigorously disputes this assertion. He appears to us to have proved that Edward I, in his charter of 1278, does not mention any charter of Edward the Confessor relative to the Cinque Ports. He also shows that we do not possess any royal charter granting privileges to the Cinque Ports as a body, anterior to that of 1278. He recognises that the charter of Edward I did not create the confederation, did nothing but sanction the relations already existing between the maritime towns of the south-east. But he asserts that "even so late as the days of John the Ports had individual relations with the crown, although their relations *inter se* were becoming of a closer character, as was illustrated by the fact that their several charters were all obtained at the same time (in 1205). Hastings alone, as yet, had rights at Yarmouth recognised : hers were the only portsmen styled "barons" by the crown." It is surprising to find a scholar like Mr. Round in error. Formal documents, which are very accessible, refute his view. I have collected, in my *Etude sur la vie et le règne de Louis VIII,* a fair number of documents concerning the Cinque Ports in the time of John Lackland and Henry III (see my index at the word Cinque Ports.) They prove that, not only did the Cinque Ports in the eyes of the contemporary chroniclers, of the Pope and of the legate, form an official confederation, but John and the counsellors of his infant son treated them as such, and did not reserve the name of barons to the inhabitants of Hastings alone. It will suffice to quote a letter patent of 26 May, 1216, in which John Lackland institutes Earl Warenne as warden of the Cinque Ports, whose "barons," moreover, had decided to take the side of Lewis of France : "Rex baronibus de Quinque Portubus. Quia nolumus quemquam alienigenam vobis capud vel magistrum prefici, mittimus ad vos dilectum nobis et fidelem W. comitem Warenniae, consanguineum nostrum, ut presit vobis ex parte nostra ad vos custodiendum et defendendum." (*Rotuli litt. Pat.* i, p. 184, col. 1). Since when had this confederation existed? I do not know whether the question can ever be settled. Mr. Round recognises that the problem is difficult, and Samuel Jeake (*Charters of the Cinque-Ports,* 1728, p. 121) already said that the origin of the Cinque-Ports and their members was a very obscure question. We cannot, in any case, discuss it with any chance of success until all the documents bearing upon it have been got together. Works such as the book—a very artistic production it may be admitted—of Mr. F. M. Hueffer (*The Cinque Ports, a historical and descriptive record,* 1900) are useless to the scholar, owing to the absence of any serious study of the sources.

conquerors created towns to secure their domination, and gave these towns French customs. This very interesting discovery was made by Miss Mary Bateson.[1]

It was thought until recently that the customs of Bristol had served as a model to a great number of English towns;[2] it was, in most of the cases, a mistake, arising from a faulty translation of the place-name Britolium. Miss Bateson has shown that at least seventeen towns of England, Wales and Ireland, perhaps twenty-five,[3] had been granted the customs and franchises of the little Norman town of Breteuil, that several of these seventeen towns—Hereford, Rhuddlan and Shrewsbury—served in their turn as models to others, had daughter towns, even grand-daughter towns. Thus Breteuil played the same part in England as Lorris or Beaumont-en-Argonne in France, or Freiburg-im-Breisgau in Germany. It was not a very ancient or very celebrated town; it first appears in history about 1060 when Duke William built a castle there; but William Fitz-Osbern, to whom the castle of Breteuil was entrusted, became one of the greatest personages of Norman England,[4] and it is to him and his powerful family that the diffusion of the customs of Breteuil is due. This diffusion took place principally in the March of Wales, and its history shows how, by

The diffusion of the customs of Breteuil

1. 'The Laws of Breteuil,' in *English Histor. Review*, xv, 1900, and xvi, 1901. Aug. de Prévost, *Mém. pour servir à l'hist. du départ. de l'Eure*, 1862, i, pp. 430 sqq., had already given useful information on this subject. See also R. Génestal, *La tenure en bourgage dans les pays régis par la coutume de Normandie*, 1900, pp. 237 sqq.

2. Mr. Gross enumerates thirty-one towns "affiliated" to Bristol (*Gild Merchant*, i, pp. 244 sqq.); eleven only, amongst these thirty-one, were so in reality.

3. Hereford, Rhuddlan, Shrewsbury, Nether Weare, Bideford, Drogheda in Meath and Drogheda Bridge, Ludlow, Rathmore, Dungarvan, Chipping Sodbury, Lichfield, Ellesmere, Burford, Ruyton, Welshpool, Llanvyllin, Preston. The eight less certain cases are those of Stratford-on-Avon, Trim, Kells, Duleek, Old Leighlin, Cashel, Kilmaclenan, Kilmeaden.

4. Stubbs, i, p. 389.

the creation of castles and of free towns the Norman
Process of barons definitively colonised and subjected
urban regions far from the centre of government
colonisation where the pressure of the royal power was
comparatively weak.   The castle was generally constructed near an already existing village; the village was
converted into a free town, or even in some cases a new
town was built beside the village.   The creation of a
market, the assured custom of the garrison, the bait of
the franchises of Breteuil, attracted settlers.   The former
inhabitants of the village continued to cultivate the land,
whilst the new population, endowed with very small
holdings, comprising, for example, a house and a garden,
gave themselves up to industry and commerce.   At times
even a third element placed itself side by side with the
two others; at Shrewsbury, for instance, there was a
colony of French merchants, who lived apart and under
a régime which had some special features.   The article
of the customs of Breteuil to which the burgesses
attached the most value was doubtless that which reduced
the maximum fine to 12 pence.   It is to be found in
the customs of many towns of Wales, Ireland, Devon,
Cornwall, etc., which did not enjoy the rest of the
franchises of Breteuil.

Thus the process of urban colonisation, employed
throughout the whole extent of France by the church,
the feudal baronage and the crown, employed also to
civilize Germany, at first by Charlemagne, then by the
emperors and princes of the twelfth and thirteenth
centuries, was also applied in England.   The " ville
neuve " is to be found there[1] with franchises borrowed
from a French prototype.

It cannot, however, be denied that the development of
the English towns had a somewhat peculiar character,—

1. See what M. Luchaire says about the 'villes neuves': *Manuel des
institutions françaises*, pp. 445—450.

Original
features of the
English towns

above all, because it was slower than on the Continent and was incomplete. The English towns never attained complete independence; during the whole of the Middle Ages they remained rather small urban groups. Must we conclude from this that the Anglo-Saxon genius was ill-adapted for city life, and was only at its ease in the organization of the village and the agricultural group?[1] We will not invoke the " genius of the race;" it is better to explain this fact by the economic conditions peculiar to mediæval England and by the extraordinary power of its monarchy.[2]

1. This is what Mr. Round says in a passage which, however, is concerned only with the Anglo-Saxon period (*Commune of London*, 1899, p. 221.)

2. It will suffice to recall the case of the most important of English towns, London, whose mediocre liberties were unceasingly at the mercy of the kings. See below.

IX.

LONDON IN THE TWELFTH CENTURY.

ACCORDING to Stubbs,[1] the charter of Henry I., granted to the Londoners in the first years of the twelfth century [2]

The charter of Henry I. profoundly altered the organisation of London. The " complex system of gild and franchise " gave place to the system of the county; the city became a county in itself, and the county of Middlesex, in which it lay, was let at farm to the Londoners by Henry I.; henceforth London had its own sheriff. But Henry I.'s favours were ephemeral; the *Pipe Roll* of 1130 bears witness to it. The suppression of such precious privileges, the disappearance of the port-reeve, the conversion of the *cnihten-gild* into a religious house, " signify, perhaps, a municipal revolution the history of which is lost."

Such a statement of the facts treats the searching studies of Mr. Round as if they had never been.[3]

It is to them that, pending the appearance of a good history of London, which does not yet exist,[4] we must

1. *Const. Hist.*, i, p. 439 sqq.; 673 sqq.

2. *Ibid.*, p. 674.

3. *The early administration of London*, in *Geoffrey de Mandeville* (1892), "Appendix P," pp. 347—373;—*London under Stephen*, in *The Commune of London* (1899), pp. 97—124. Stubbs quotes (p. 440, note 1) the first of these two articles for a detail concerning a misreading of the charter of Henry I, and he adds that "the whole history of London at this period is treated there," but in spite of this admission, he has not rectified his certainly erroneous interpretation of the charter of Henry I.

4. We await with impatience the volumes dealing with London, which are to form a special series in the *Victoria History* of the counties. Quite recently there has appeared the first volume of a description of London in the Middle Ages by Sir Walter Besant (*Mediæval London*, 1906, i). There is scarcely a mention in this first volume of the municipal institutions which are to be studied in vol. ii. Sir Walter Besant's work is unprovided with any notes or *apparatus criticus*.

look for an exact and intelligible interpretation of the charter of Henry I.

" Sciatis me concessisse civibus meis Londoniarum tenendum Middlesex ad firmam pro ccc libris ad compotum, ipsis et haeredibus suis, de me et haeredibus meis, ita quod ipsi cives ponent vicecomitem qualem voluerint de se ipsis." [1]

Several scholars, notably Freeman,—Stubbs has not taken sides clearly on this point—have thought that by this clause Henry I. gave Middlesex in some sort to the Londoners, made of it a district subject to London, in its fiscal relations. Mr. Round has shown, that *Middlesex* here signifies London and Middlesex which surrounds it, that London and Middlesex formed but a single unit for the farm of taxation, and that this state of things, far from having been created by the charter of Henry I., existed long before. It was natural, indeed, that the smallest of the English counties should form one body with the greatest of English towns, which it contained. It is also a mistake to believe that the office of sheriff was created by the charter of Henry. The sheriff (*shire-reeve*) existed before, but, as here the town (*port*) was more important than the county (*shire*), that officer was called the *port-reeve* and not the *shire-reeve*. The *vicecomes* is no other than the *port-reeve* of London, who was, perhaps, called *shire-reeve*, sheriff when dealing with the affairs of Middlesex. The title of *port-reeve* disappeared in the 12th century, but not the office. [2]

Henry I., then, neither constituted London a county, **Real object of the Charter** nor subjected Middlesex to London, nor created the office of sheriff of London. [3]

1. *Select Charters*, p. 108.

2. As for the "conversion of the *cnihten-gild* into a religious house" accepted by Stubbs, Coote, and Loftie, it is, Mr. Round has shown, pure imagination.

3. Was the office of justiciar of London, on the contrary, a novelty? Henry I. says in his charter : " . . . ipsi cives ponent . . . . justitiarium qualem voluerint de seipsis, ad custodiendum placita coronae meae et eadem placitanda, et nullus alius erit justitiarius super ipsos homines

[handwritten margin note:] Henry I's charter did not grant Middlesex to London; for purposes of taxation they were identical before: it did not create a sheriff of London, but gave London the right to pay taxes directly to the King — Round.

But the Londoners, who had evidently suffered from the exactions of the royal sheriffs, by the charter in question obtained the entire disposal of the office, in other words they paid the farm of the City and of Middlesex to the king themselves.

In addition, the farm, which Henry I. had increased to £500, was brought down to the previous figure of £300.

There is nothing to compel us to believe that the charter of Henry I., whose date is unknown, is earlier **No corporate unity** than the *Pipe Roll* of 1130, which bears witness to an organisation much less advantageous to the citizens; it was this unfavourable organisation that in all probability the charter granted by Henry remedied. But there was still nothing, it seems, in the capital, which resembled a municipality;[1] as Stubbs says, London was nothing but an " assemblage of little communities, manors, parishes, ecclesias-

---

Londoniarum." Mr. Round asserts that this office, which arose from a dismemberment of the sheriffdom, was, as far as London is concerned, created by the charter of Henry I (*Geoffrey de Mandeville*, pp. 106 sqq. and Append. P, p. 373). Nevertheless Mr. Round has himself republished a charter of 1141, in which King Stephen confers on Geoffrey de Mandeville "*justicias* et vicecomitatum de Londonia et de Middlesexa in feodo et hereditate *eadem firma qua Gaufridus de Mannavilla avus suus eas tenuit, scilicet pro CCC libris*" (*Ibidem*, pp. 141-142). The office existed, therefore, at the end of the preceding century (cf. *ibidem*, p. 373), unless we assume that the charter of 1141 mentions separately two offices which were still united in one in the time of Geoffrey de Mandeville the grandfather. We should like, however, to draw attention to the fact that this is pure hypothesis, and that there is nothing in the charter of Henry I. to show that the office was a new one. This office is several times mentioned in the collection of London municipal documents, contained in the additional MS. 14, 252, which Miss Bateson has analysed in the *English Historical Review*. Unfortunately, these documents are for the most part undated. The justiciar is there called *justicia* in Latin, *justise* in French. (*English Historical Review*, xvii, 1902, pp. 707, 711.)

1. Dr. Liebermann has, indeed, drawn attention to a phrase in the little tract entitled *De injusta vexatione Willelmi Dunelmensis*, of which Stubbs had occasion to make use for another purpose (See Stubbs, i, p. 476). We should mention there of the "meliores duodecim cives" of London, and it may be asked whether there is not a reference here to a body of twelve notables governing London, as early as the end of the 11th century (Cf. Mary Bateson, in *English Historical Review*, xvii, 1902, p. 730, note 105.)

tical jurisdictions and gilds," and each of these organisms had a life of its own. The corporate unity of London was prepared for only by some common institutions : I mean the financial system of the royal farm, the *folkmoot*,—an assembly of little importance which had met from time immemorial,—and above all the weekly court of Danish origin, the *husting*. The misfortunes and anarchy of Stephen's reign showed the value and necessity of this corporate unity, without however bringing about its definitive realisation.

The Londoners, who had taken part in the election of Stephen, and who, during the disorder of the civil war,

The "communio" of 1141

saw the monarchical power dissolve and the king's peace disappear, were too proud, too careful for the security of their persons and their property, not to aspire to the unity alone capable of securing their independence and rendering them redoubtable. They were in constant relations with the communities of the Continent. The idea came quite naturally to them of imitating these. It appears that in 1141, the year in which they made a *conspiratio* to drive out the Empress Matilda, they formed a sort of sworn commune; William of Malmesbury speaks of a *communio* and says that barons had been received into this association.[1]

There would seem, then, to have been a revolutionary movement in London analogous to those which agitated certain towns of the Continent. But it very often happened that the leagues formed under oath, in French or German towns had no lasting result.[2]

---

1. "Feria quarta venerunt Londonienses, et, in concilium introducti, causam suam eatenus egerunt ut dicerent missos se a communione quam vocant Londoniarum, non certamina sed preces offerre, ut dominus suus rex de captione liberaretur. Hoc omnes barones, qui in eorum communionem jamdudum recepti fuerant, summopere flagitare a domino legato." (Will. of Malmesbury, *Hist. Novella*, Ed. Stubbs, ii, p. 576.) Cf. the account given by Stubbs, *Const. Hist.*, i, p. 442.

2. For example, the league formed in 958 by the people of Cambray to prevent their bishop from returning to their town : "Cives Cameraci male consulti *conspirationem* multo tempore susurratam et diu desideratam

This was what took place in the case of the "communio" of 1141, whatever may have been its precise character.

Far from granting new privileges to the Londoners, who had just rendered him a splendid service, Stephen was, in fact, obliged by circumstances to **King Stephen and London** favour the powerful Geoffrey de Mandeville at their expense, and to take from them even the advantages which had been granted to them by Henry I., or at least those which they valued most. As early as Christmas of this same year 1141, the offices of sheriff and justiciar of London were conferred on or rather restored by Stephen to, the house of Mandeville, which had already enjoyed them, at the end of the preceding century, in return for a farm of £300.[1]

In the reign of Henry II., the sheriffs of London and of Middlesex are named by the king, and the farm rises to the figure of £500 or even more. **Henry II. and London** The office of justiciar, doubtless incompatible with the circuits of the itinerant justices, disappears. The charter of 1155 marks a reaction from the charter of Henry I. The reign of the most powerful sovereign, of the most despotic statesman perhaps who had yet governed the English had just begun, and the son of Matilda could not easily pardon the Londoners either for the support they had given Stephen against the empress, or for their aspirations to independence.

juraverunt *communiam*. Adeo sunt inter se sacramento conjuncti, quod nisi factam concederet *conjurationem*, denegarent universi introitum Cameraci reversuro pontifici." This phrase of the *Gesta episcoporum Cameracensium* (*Monum. Germ.* SS. vii, p. 498) recalls the *communio* and the *conspiratio* of London in 1141. But it proves (*nisi factam concederet conjurationem*) that the Cambresians demanded liberties, while we know absolutely nothing of the end aimed at by the *communio* of the Londoners, and their *conspiratio* of the month of June 1141 seems to have had for its sole object the expulsion of Matilda.

1. Sir Walter Besant does not seem to have been acquainted with this charter of Stephen in favour of the Mandevilles. (Cf. *Mediæval London*, i, p. 4.)

Exactly half-a-century after the episode of 1141, when Henry II. was dead, when Richard was fighting in the Holy Land, and civil troubles were beginning again in England, the Londoners took advantage of the conflict between William Longchamp and John Lackland to renew the attempt to establish a commune. This time, they succeeded, and John took an oath to the *communa* of London on the 8th of October.[1] It was a real commune, a "seigneurie collective populaire" in the French fashion. The famous invective of Richard of Devizes proves this fact very clearly.[2] The commune of London doubtless organised itself immediately. In any case,—we learn this from a text which Dr. Liebermann had pointed out and Mr. Round first made full use of,—as early as 1193, it had a mayor. At that date, indeed, the members of the commune of London swear to remain faithful to Richard, who is a prisoner in Germany; they swear also to adhere to the commune, and obey the mayor of the city of London and the *skivini* (*échevins*) of the commune, and give consideration to the mayor and *skivini* and other *probi homines* who shall be with them.[3]

Stubbs, who was not acquainted with this document,

The commune of 1191

The mayor of London

The Londoners finally established a commune on the fall of Wm Longchamp, 1191.

1. See the very brief account in Stubbs, i, p. 673.
2. "Concessa est ipsa die et instituta communia Londoniensium, in quam universi regni magnates et ipsi etiam ipsius provinciae episcopi jurare coguntur. Nunc primum in indulta sibi conjuratione regno regem deesse cognovit Londonia, quam nec rex ipse Ricardus, nec praedecessor et pater ejus Henricus pro mille millibus marcarum argenti fieri permisisset. Quanta quippe mala ex conjuratione proveniant ex ipsa poterit diffinitione perpendi, quae talis est : communia est tumor plebis, timor regni, tepor sacerdotii" (Ed. Howlett in *Chronicles of the reigns of Stephen, etc.* (Rolls Ser.), iii, p. 416.)
3. "*Sacramentum commune tempore regis Ricardi quando detentus erat Alemaniam* (sic.).—Quod fidem portabunt domino regi Ricardo de vita sua et de membris et de terreno honore suo contra omnes homines et feminas qui vivere possunt aut mori et quod pacem suam servabunt et adjuvabunt servare, et quod communam tenebunt et obedientes erunt maiori civitatis Lond[onie] et skivin[is] ejusdem commune in fide regis et quod sequentur et tenebunt considerationem maioris et skivinorum et aliorum proborum hominum qui cum illis erunt salvo honore Dei et sancte Ecclesie et fide domini regis Ricardi et salvis per omnia libertatibus civitatis Lond[onie]." (Round, *Commune of London*, pp. 235-236.)

had divined the character of the revolution of 1191. He
Character of this revolution according to Stubbs notes the French origin of the office of mayor, and of the commune. He only touches lightly on the question in his *Constitutional History*. But, in one of the substantial notices with which. he has accompanied his *Select Charters,* he writes : " The mayoralty of London dates from the earliest years of Richard I., probably from the foundation of that *communa* which was confirmed on the occasion of William Longchamp's downfall. The name of that officer, as well as that of the *communa* itself, is French. That the incorporation under this form was held to imply very considerable municipal independence may be inferred from the fact that one of the charges brought by William Fitz-Osbert against Richard Fitz-Osbert, was that he had not forbidden the saying : *quodcunque eat vel veniat quod nunquam habeant Londonienses alium regem quam majorem Londoniarum.*" [1]

The influence of French institutions on the establishment of this commune of London is not matter of doubt, any more than is the high degree of **Hypotheses of Mr. Round** independence to which the citizens laid claim. It is more than probable that they had chosen their mayor themselves. But what are the *skivini* and *probi homines* who appear in the oath of the commune in 1193 ? The mention which is made of them has suggested to Mr. Round a very ingenious hypothesis. It is that the constitution of London was modelled upon the *Établissements* of Rouen[2] and that London, like Rouen, had a council of twelve *skivini* and twelve other persons (the *duodecim consultores* of Rouen, the *alii probi homines* of the oath of 1193), to administer justice. And, in fact, adds Mr. Round, we

1. *Select Charters*, 8th edition, p. 308.
2. Mr. Round makes a correction of M. Giry's book on the *Établissements* of Rouen and proves that they are anterior to the year 1183 (*Commune of London*, pp. 247—251.)

G

have the text of an oath sworn to King John in 1205—
1206 by twenty-four persons charged with the administration of justice in London; these twenty-four are not
the aldermen, who are simply heads of wards. The
twenty-four can only have been councillors elected by
the mass of the burgesses.

**And of
Mr. Adams**
Mr. G. B. Adams has sought to complete and follow up Mr. Round's hypothesis.[1]

According to him, the commune created in 1191 was
a commune in the technical sense, a " seigneurie
collective," a vassal of the king, like the great French
communes. King Richard did not allow London thus
to quit his demesne, and by becoming his vassal escape
the domanial claims and took this privilege away from
it as soon as he returned, whilst leaving it its mayor and
its *skivini*. London thus ceases to be a commune until
the day when John is forced to seek its support. By
article 12 of the Great Charter he formally recognises
the feudal character of the city, for he admits that it
owes to him the *auxilium*, that is to say the feudal aid,
the aid of the nobles. A document of the reign of
Henry III. shows, in fact, that London claimed only to
give the king an aid, and refuse to pay the tallage;[2]
this pretension was however rejected by the counsellors
of Henry III. London did not succeed in obtaining a
lasting recognition of its legal right to a commune.

We cannot subscribe wholly to either the theory of
Mr. Round or that of Mr. Adams. Miss Mary
Bateson has studied from beginning to end

**No filiation
with Rouen**
the collection of municipal documents in
which Mr. Round found the oath of 1193,
and has discovered in it texts which render untenable

1. *London and the Commune*, in *English Historical Review*, xix, 1904,
pp. 702 sqq.
2. Mr. Adams contents himself with analysing this important text.
There is some advantage in reading it *in extenso*; it is printed by Madox,
Exchequer, i, p. 712, note a (edition of 1769). See the abstract and
fragments of it we give below.

the hypothesis of a filiation between London and Rouen.[1] We see, in fact, there that the aldermen sat in the husting, that they declared the law there,[2] and beyond doubt the twenty-four who are mentioned in the text of 1205–6 are aldermen, and not a self-styled council of twelve *skivini* and twelve *probi homines*. For the rest, it is quite likely that the *skivini* mentioned in the text of 1193—without their number being specified—are simply the twenty-four aldermen; *skivini* was an exotic term which a scribe may have used to designate the aldermen; and it is remarkable that it is not found afterwards, in any text relating to London. As for the *probi homines*—whose number Mr. Round, with no more reason than in the case of the *skivini,* fixes at *twelve,*—they were, in the most vague and general sense, notables, who advised and aided the mayor, and on occasion this term doubtless served to denote the aldermen themselves. There were *probi homines* sitting in the husting,[3] and it is not surprising that the burgesses, in 1193, swear to respect them; it is noticeable, moreover, that they do not swear to obey them.[4]

We shall only, therefore, admit that London formed itself into a commune in 1191, and that it had—immediately doubtless—a mayor. We

Richard certainly did not recognise the commune

shall also admit with Mr. Round and Mr. Adams that Richard Cœur-de-Lion suppressed the commune (or at least that he took no account of the oath of 1191),

[margin note: Richard I did not recognise the commune,]

1. Mary Bateson, *A London Municipal Collection of the reign of John,* in *English Historical Review,* xvii, 1902, pp. 480 sqq., 707 sqq.
2. "E les aldremans dirunt si le rei deit aveir le plai u le vescunte . . . Les aldermans en durunt dreit." (*Ibidem,* p. 493.)
3. ". . . . Dunc deit le veskunte prendre quatre prudomes dedenz les quatre bancs del husteng . . . ." (*Ibidem,* p. 493).) Respecting these "quatre bancs," see Mary Bateson, *Boroughs Customs,* ii, 1906, p. cxlvii.
4. *Eng. Hist. Rev.,* xvii, pp. 510-511. On pages 727-728 of the same volume Miss Bateson prints a text which fully confirms her view. "Item de omni redditu forinsecorum capiatur de singulis libris xiid. exceptis redditibus ecclesiasticis. Item ad hanc pecuniam colligendam et recipiendam eligantur iiii *probi ac discreti homines* de qualibet custodia." *Probi homnes* is used in no more technical or precise sense than *discreti homines.*

while maintaining a mayor, who kept his office for life. John Lackland, indeed, at his accession, granted to the Londoners their old privilege of holding the sheriffdom of London and Middlesex, for a farm of 300 pounds; this privilege for which the Londoners paid King John a sum of 3,000 marks, they would have had no need to buy if they had been at that time an independent commune, protected, by the liberties it had won, against the royal sheriffs and the financial pressure of the crown. Moreover, in the three charters granted to the Londoners at this period there is no mention made of the commune.

Was the commune of London restored afterwards by John Lackland, when he had need of the support of **Did John** the inhabitants? Such is, we have seen, **recognise it?** the opinion of Mr. Adams based on article 12 of the Great Charter and a document of the time of Henry III. Mr. MacKechnie, for his part, is of opinion that the charter of the 9th May, 1215, granting to the Londoners the right of electing their mayor annually, is an official recognition of the commune.[1] Let us look at these documents more closely, and, if possible, throw light on them by others.

Miss Bateson discovered a list of nine articles, which seems to be a summary of a petition presented by the **The Nine** Londoners before the granting of the **Articles** charter of the 9th of May, 1215; the annual mayoralty is mentioned;[2] There is no mention of a commune; no mention is made of it either in the charter of the 9th of May. By this last document,[3] John only grants to his " barons " of the city of **The charter of** London the right to elect every year from **9 May, 1215.** their own number a mayor " faithful to the

1. "The charter of May, 1215, by officially recognizing the mayor, placed the commune over which he presided on a legal footing. The revolutionary civic constitution, sworn to in 1191, was now confirmed." (MacKechnie, *Magna Carta*, 1905, p. 289.)

2. "De majore habendo, de anno in annum, per folkesmot, et quod primum juret." (*English Histor. Review*, xvii, 1902, p. 726; art 7).

3. *Select Charters*, pp. 314-315 (8th edition).

king, discreet and suitable for the government of the
city " who is to be " presented " to the king, or, in
his absence, to the justiciar, and swear fealty to him.
At the end of a year the Londoners might keep the same
mayor, or change him. The liberties of London are
confirmed in vague terms.[1] Unquestionably the right
of electing the mayor annually was extremely important,
and this right was actually exercised by the Londoners.
But it cannot be claimed that it was sufficient to constitute
a commune in the French sense of the word.

As for article 12 of the Great Charter, it is obscure
and we may be allowed to quote it in its exact form :

London and the Great Charter " Nullum scutagium vel auxilium ponatur
in regno nostro, nisi per commune consilium
regni nostri, nisi ad corpus nostrum
redimendum, et primogenitum filium nostrum militem
faciendum, et ad filiam nostram primogenitam semel
maritandam, et ad hec non fiat nisi racionabile auxilium ;
simili modo fiat de auxiliis de civitate London."
Article 13 goes on :[2] " Et civitas London. habeat omnes
antiquas libertates et liberas consuetudines suas, tam per
terras quam per aquas.   Preterea volumus et concedimus
quod omnes alie civitates et burgi et ville et portus
habeant omnes libertates et liberas consuetudines suas."[3]
By article 12, John Lackland pledges himself not to levy
any scutage or aid beyond the three occasions provided
for by feudal law, without the consent of the assembly
of tenants-in-chief, and the aid in these three cases is
to be levied on a reasonable scale.   But what does the

1. "Concessimus etiam eisdem baronibus nostris et carta nostra con-
firmavimus quod habeant bene et in pace, libere, quiete et integre, omnes
libertates suas quibus hactenus usi sunt, tam in civitate Londoniarum
quam extra, et tam in aquis quam in terris, et omnibus aliis locis, salva
nobis chamberlengeria nostra." These last words signify that the pur-
veyors of the king's household shall have the right of making their
choice, first of all, from the goods brought in by foreign merchants.

2. It is not without interest to remember that this division into articles
does not exist in the original.

3. Bémont, *Chartes des Libertés Anglaises*, p. 29.

obscure phrase relative to the aids of the city of London mean ? Must we conclude from it with Mr. Adams that John Lackland identified the aids of London with the feudal aids, and thus recognised its character of a "seigneurie collective populaire ?"

Nor did John.

We do not think so. In order to understand this phrase we must go back to article 32 of the *Articuli Baronum*, a petition presented by the barons to John Lackland some days before the granting of the Great Charter : " Ne scutagium vel auxilium ponatur in regno, nisi per commune consilium regni, nisi ad corpus regis redimendum, et primogenitum filium suum militem faciendum, et filiam suam primogenitam semel maritandam ; et ad hoc fiat rationabile auxilium. *Simili modo fiat de taillagiis et auxiliis de civitate London.* et de aliis civitatibus que inde habent libertates, et ut civitas London. plene habeat antiquas libertates et liberas consuetudines suas tam per aquas, quam per terras."[1]

London and the Petition of the Barons

The Londoners were not pressing for the recognition of their commune; they simply sought to avoid tallage, not to insist that, as a commune they paid only an aid

Mr. Adams declares that this article of the petition of the barons was badly drafted, whilst the corresponding article of the Great Charter was drafted with care. We believe, on the contrary, that the article of the petition of the barons alone represents the precise wishes of the Londoners. They desired a guarantee against royal arbitrariness, and did not wish any longer to have to pay ruinous taxes, either in the form of *tallage* or in the form of *aids*,—an extremely elastic term, which had very diverse meanings and was in no wise reserved for the feudal aid.[2]

What the Londoners wanted.

S.B. Adams' theory that Magna Carta recognized the corporation of London is thus untenable.

1. Bémont, *op. cit.*, p. 19.
2. The author of the *Dialogue concerning the Exchequer*, ii, c. xiii (Edition of Hughes, Crump and Johnson, p. 145), speaks formally of the *donum* or *auxilium* of the towns : "de auxiliis vel donis civitatum seu burgorum." And, in fact, in the first half of the 12th century, when the Danegeld was still collected, the sum furnished by Middlesex was paid under the name of *Danegeld*, that paid by London was paid under the name of *donum* or *auxilium*. See on this point Round, *Commune of London*, pp. 257 sqq. We may read in Stubbs (i, p. 620, note 2), a writ of 1207, in which John demands an *auxilium* from the archdeacons

The tallage was the tax which bore upon the inhabitants of the royal demesne, and the towns possessing a royal charter were considered as forming part of the demesne. The aid was in theory a gift made to the king, and the townsmen did not escape from the ill-defined obligation to this gratuity, any more than the clergy or the nobility. The Londoners feared the tallage even more than the aid.[1] A text to which attention has never been paid until now proves this. In the list of nine articles, of which I was speaking just now, I read as follows: " De omnibus taillagiis delendis nisi per communem assensum regni et civitatis." Thus, before obtaining their private charter of the 9th of May, the Londoners already demanded that they might not be subjected to the tallage without the consent of the *regnum,* that is to say, evidently, the assembly of the tenants-in-chief. The silence of the charter of the 9th of May proves that John did not wish to give up any part of his prerogative upon this point. The following month the barons, who had great obligations towards the townsmen of the realm, and particularly towards the Londoners, included in their petition article 32, which secured London and the towns having the same liberties as London against the abuses of zeal for the interests of the royal treasury,—in so far as the consent of an assembly of barons could be a security. Comparison of the petition of the barons and the Great Charter shows that in this question, as in many others, John Lackland exacted a compromise.[2] He refused to put any other town in the position of London, and even to London he only granted a derisive satisfaction.

John's illusory concession

of the realm, and expresses the desire that the rest of the clergy may be influenced by the example of the archdeacons to pay an *auxilium* also. The word was therefore used in a very wide sense. Cf. Stubbs, i, pp. 626—628.

1. They had just paid, in the year 1214-15, a tallage of 2,000 marks : "Anno ejusdem Johannis sextodecimo, talliati fuerunt praedicti cives Londoniae ad duo millia marcarum." (Madox, *Hist of Exchequer,* i, p. 712, note a.)

2. This is well put by Mr. MacKechnie, *Magna Carta,* pp. 277 sqq.

The suppression of the words *de taillagiis* allowed him to tallage the Londoners at his pleasure; on these conditions he could do without their *auxilia*. Such, in our opinion, is the true explanation of article 12 of the Great Charter.

The argument which Mr. Adams draws from the text published by Madox is more specious. It may be asked why the Londoners were so particular about paying an *auxilium* and not a *tallagium*.[1] But the context supplies a very simple answer to this question. Henry III. levies a tallage of three thousand marks on the Londoners. They refuse to pay it and offer an aid of two thousand marks.[2] They are told that they may pay, if they wish, a composition of three thousand marks in place of the tallage,[3] but if they refuse the tallage shall be assessed on the town in the form of a capitation. The Londoners still resist, and then arises the dispute over the use of the word *tallagium;* the inquest proves the baselessness of their pretension, they recognise themselves as tallageable and pay the three thousand marks. For them it was clearly a question of not paying in its entirety the large sum demanded by the king, and, as they knew well that they could not discuss the amount of a tallage, they had hit on this expedient of saying that they were not tallageable, and of offering an "aid" of two thousand marks only. For an aid is, professedly, a voluntary gift to the sovereign, and it is recognised by the king's officers that the assessment

Why London claimed exemption from tallage

1. "Et cum contencio esset, utrum hoc dici deberet tallagium vel auxilium, rex scrutari fecit rotulos suos, utrum ipsi aliquid dederunt regi vel antecessoribus suis nomine tallagii. . . ." An inquest proved that the Londoners had paid a tallage of 2,000 marks in 1214-1215, and several tallages in the reign of Henry III. "Postea in crastino . . . . venerunt praedicti Radulfus major et cives et recognoverunt se esse talliabiles." (Madox, *op. cit.* i, p. 712, note a.)

2. "Rex petebat ab eis tria millia marcarum nomine tallagii, et illi . . . optulerunt regi duo millia marcarum nomine auxilii, et dixerunt praecise quod plus non poterunt dare nec darent."

3. "Finem trium millium marcarum pro tallagio."

cannot be left to his arbitrary discretion.[1] The king was not particular about the name provided he had the thing, and he offered to abandon the tallage if they would pay him its equivalent; as the Londoners did not comply and haggled over the terms, he forced them to recognize that they were tallageable. They never dreamed of asserting that they constituted a commune and that because of this they owed nothing but a feudal aid; there is nothing of the kind in the text, and Mr. Adams's argument will not hold water.

Not only was the " Commune of London " not recognised by John Lackland, but the burgesses did not even show any desire for such recognition. **London did not demand the recognition of the commune** They asked for nothing of the sort in the nine articles, or in the petition of the barons. I will add that such a claim is equally absent from their demands, some months later, when Lewis of France, son of Philip Augustus, landed in England, and this fact appears to me decisive. The Londoners were the most faithful allies of Lewis, his allies from first to last. The pretender could have refused them nothing. Now, there is no question of the recognition of the commune either in the engagements he entered into with them on his arrival nor in the negotiations and stipulations of the peace which preceded his definitive departure.[2]

1. In a very interesting passage, which Mr. Adams has not had present in his memory, the author of the *Dialogue concerning the Exchequer* (Bk. ii, c. xiii, Edn. of Hughes, Crump and Johnson, p. 145) discusses the case in which the *donum vel auxilium* of the towns was imposed by the officers of the king in the form of a capitation (observe that this is the procedure with which Henry III threatens the Londoners, if they do not give way), and the case in which it consists of a round sum, offered by the burgesses, and accepted as " principe digna." In the eyes of the author of the *Dialogue*, there is no reason for reserving for this offer " worthy of the prince" the name of *auxilium*, and calling *tallagium* only the tax imposed in the form of a capitation. In the thirteenth century, men become more subtle, the burgesses try to make distinctions to their profit; but they have no idea of claiming that London ought to be treated as a feudal person, nor do they invoke article 12 of the Great Charter to prove it.

2. See my *Etude sur la vie et le règne de Louis VIII*, especially pp. 102 and 160 (Cf. the word *Londres* in the index). According to the

We must neither exaggerate or depreciate the status of London at this period. The city was not a commune in the French sense of the word; it had only been so for a very brief space, during the absence of Richard Cœur de Lion. It was not bound to the king by that mutual oath which, according to the historians was characteristic of the French *seigneurie collective populaire* : this bilateral oath had only been taken in 1191, and since the return of Richard Cœur-de-Lion there had been no longer question of anything but the oath taken by the burgesses or their mayor. The city had not, in the matter of finance and justice, the independence of the popular republics of the Continent.[1] Nevertheless it was very powerful, and rival parties disputed its alliance. Its inhabitants were " barons." *Londonienses, qui sunt quasi optimates, pro magnitudine civitatis,* said William of Malmesbury, who wrote in the time of King Stephen; since that time, thanks to the difficulties of the reign of Richard I. and the crisis of 1215, London had gradually gained one of the principal municipal liberties, that of having an annually elected mayor. And perhaps, after all, it is puerile to investigate whether London in 1215 was or was not a commune; the Londoners of that day did not trouble themselves about it; and without doubt we attach too much importance to words which we have made technical terms for the convenience of our historical studies.

Actual status of London

account of several chroniclers, Lewis, on his arrival, 3 June, 1216, received the 'homage' of the citizens, and in return promised to give back to the Londoners good laws : "Juravit quod *singulis eorum* bonas leges redderet, simul et amissas hereditates." But the reference here is only to the mutual pledge quite natural under the circumstances, and not to the oath of the commune. See the passages quoted *ibidem*, p. 102, note 2.

1. Four times at least in eleven years, Henry III seized the town of London into his hands, notably for false judgement in the husting (Pollock and Maitland, *Hist. of English Law*, i, p. 668.)

X.

THE TWO TRIALS OF JOHN LACKLAND.

ACCORDING to the narrative of Stubbs, John Lackland was twice condemned as contumacious by the court **Narrative of** of Philip Augustus—in 1202 and in 1203. **Stubbs** After his first condemnation, in 1202, his nephew Arthur, " taking advantage of the confusion, raised a force and besieged his grandmother in the castle of Mirabel, where he was captured by John, and, after some mysterious transactions, he disappeared finally on the 3rd of April, 1203. Philip, who believed with the rest of the world that John had murdered him, summoned him again to be tried on the accusation made by the barons of Brittany. Again John was contumacious, and this time Philip himself undertook to enforce the sentence of the court " and conquered Normandy.[1] It is singular that so careful a scholar as Stubbs should have summarised these celebrated events with so much negligence;[2] it is still more surprising that he took no account, in the successive editions of his book, of the opinion accepted and expressed, for a score of years, by all the

1. *Const. Hist.*, i, p. 556.
2. To speak only of quite well known and indisputable facts. Stubbs appears not to know that, as early as the month of June 1202, long before the death of Arthur, and in execution of the first sentence of the court of France, Philip-Augustus had taken up arms and invaded Normandy. If he had narrated these events with more exactitude he would, no doubt, have been led to see the improbability of the view that there were two condemnations, which M. Bémont has so thoroughly refuted. In the otherwise very remarkable preface, written for his edition of the *Historical collections of Walter of Coventry* (Rolls Series; ii, p. xxxii, note 3) he only noted that the earliest mention of the condemnation of 1203 was to be found in the manifesto launched by Lewis of France in 1216.

French, German and English scholars, with one exception, who have given their opinion on the alleged trial of April, 1203. M. Bémont demonstrated in 1884, by the most cogent arguments, that the condemnation of John Lackland in 1203 for the murder of Arthur was a fable, invented by the court of France in 1216, in order to justify the pretensions of Lewis of France to the crown of England.[1] The attempt made in 1899 by M. Guilhiermoz to refute the thesis of M. Bémont has not met with acceptance.[2] We have examined and contested it on a previous occasion. We will content ourselves with quoting the views of two scholars who

The now accepted opinion upon the second trial

1. *De Johanne cognomine sine Terra Angliae rege Lutetiae Parisiorum anno 1202 condemnato*, 1884; French edition : *De la Condemnation de Jean sans Terre par la cour des pairs de France en 1202* in the *Revue Historique*, xxxii, 1886. Cf. Ch. Petit-Dutaillis, *Etude sur la vie et le règne de Louis VIII*, 1894, pp. 77 sqq. M. Guilhiermoz remarks that the conclusions of M. Bémont "appear to have been universally accepted," and he quotes MM. Ch. V. Langlois, Beautemps-Beaupré, Luchaire, Lot, etc.

2. Guilhiermoz, *Les deux condemnations de Jean sans Terre par la cour de Philippe-Auguste*, in *Bibl. de l'Ecole des Chartes*, 1899. Cf. his controversy with M. Bémont in the same volume, and with MM. Petit-Dutaillis and G. Monod, in *Rev. Historique*, lxxi and lxxii (1899—1900), and a new article by him in the *Nouv. Rev. hist. de droit français et étranger* (1904), p. 786 sqq. I am bound to say that on a reperusal of the article in which I refuted M. Guilhiermoz's thesis, my only regret is that I did not put my conclusion more strongly. For the rest, M. Guilhiermoz has found no supporters. See a luminous summary of the question by M. Luchaire, *Séances et Travaux de l'Acad. des Sc. Morales*, liii, 1900 ; F. Lot, *Fidèles ou vassaux* (1904), pp. 89, note 3, 223 sqq. ; R. Holtzmann, *Der Prozess gegen Johann ohne Land und die Anfänge des französischen Pairhofes*, in the *Historische Zeitschrift*, Neue Folge, lix. (1905). M. J. Lehmann, *Johann ohne Land*, in the *Historische Studien* published by E. Ebering, Pt. 45, 1904, goes beyond M. Bémont's thesis and puts forth the singular view that the documents of 1216, in which the trial of 1203 is referred to, are not authentic. I am only acquainted with the summary of this article given by M. Holtzmann, *op. cit.*, p. 32, n. 3. In England, Sir James Ramsay (*The Angevin Empire*, 1903, pp. 393 and 397) does not believe in the condemnation of 1203; but he thinks there was a citation; he interprets the documents quite wrongly and obscures the question instead of throwing light on it. An American scholar, Mr. G. B. Adams, entrusted with the treatment of this period in the *Political History of England* (ii, 1905), declares, p. 399, that he is not convinced by M. Guilhiermoz. So, too, Miss Kate Norgate in the article referred to below, and in her *John Lackland* (1902), pp. 91–92; as we shall see, Miss Norgate goes farther than M. Bémont, and assuredly much too far.

not having been brought into the controversy by M. Guilhiermoz, have expressed an opinion the impartiality of which no one will dispute. M. Luchaire declares that "he adheres until further proof is forthcoming to the conclusions of M. Bémont;" quite recently M. Holtzmann stated that the vehement polemic of M. Guilhiermoz has made no impression; it appears to him to be based rather on "a lawyer's argument than on a critical examination of the sources."

In a work devoted to English institutions I cannot dwell any longer on this point, and Stubbs' excuse is just this, that it is a matter of little importance for the subject of which he is treating whether M. Bémont is right or wrong as far as concerns the reality of the second trial of John Lackland.

But it is important to know whether M. Bémont was right in believing in the reality of the first trial; the loss of Normandy had such consequences in the constitutional history of England that it is a matter of interest, even here, to determine whether it was the result of a sentence of the court of France. The publication of M.

Miss Kate Norgate's theory respecting the first trial

Bémont's article did not affect the belief that Normandy was confiscated by legal process; only the date or dates of the confiscation were matters of controversy. But a new theory has grafted itself on that of M. Bémont. According to an article published in 1900 by Miss Kate Norgate [1] John Lackland was no more condemned by the court of Philip Augustus for refusing to redress the wrongs he had inflicted on the Poitevin barons, than for having put to death his nephew Arthur, and the "alleged condemnation" of 1202 was invented in 1204-5 by Philip Augustus, in order to overcome the scruples of the Norman clergy and justify the conquest of

---

1. *The alleged condemnation of King John by the Court of France in 1202*, in *Transactions of the Royal Historical Society*, New series, xiv, 1900, pp. 53—67.

Normandy. It seems to me expedient to examine this theory closely.

Miss Norgate's argument is as follows. Five contemporary documents narrate the citation of John Lackland before the court of France in 1202 : the French chronicles of Rigord and Guillaume le Breton, the English chronicles of Gervase of Canterbury and Ralph of Coggeshall, and finally a letter addressed by Pope Innocent III. to John Lackland on the 31st of October, 1203. Roger of Wendover does not speak of the citation at all.[1] And the later chroniclers who accepted the discredited trial of 1203, are silent as to that of 1202. The five documents mentioned above supplement one another and present no contradiction amongst themselves, as far as concerns the citation, and the relations of the two kings before the trial; but Ralph of Coggeshall alone declares that John Lackland was condemned by default,[2] and the alleged sentence of 1202 rests in reality on his single testimony. It is improbable that this abbot of an obscure monastery in Essex was better informed than Gervase of Canterbury, Rigord, Guillaume le

1. I do not quite understand why Miss Norgate limits her study to six documents in all, including Roger of Wendover. Robert of Auxerre is a contemporary of the events and his testimony has great value; he does not speak of a citation either, but he says nothing to prevent us from believing in one. See the passage in *Historiens de France*, xviii, p. 266.

2. "Tandem vero curia regis Franciae adunata adjudicavit regem Angliae tota terra sua privandum, quam hactenus de regibus Franciae ipse et progenitores sui tenuerant, eo quod fere omnia servitia eisdem terris debita per longum jam tempus facere contempserant, nec domino suo fere in aliquibus obtemperare volebant." (R. de Coggeshale, *Chronicon Anglicanum*, ed. Stevenson, p. 136). It will be observed that the sentence is based upon the faults committed by *John and by his ancestors*, towards their suzerains the kings of France. This, it seems to me, has escaped the scholars who have quoted this passage; M. Bémont (*op. cit.*, p. 54 and p. 307) and M. Luchaire (*Hist. de France*, publiée sous la direction de M. Lavisse, iii, 1re partie, 1901, pp. 128-129) translate it inaccurately. Sir James Ramsay (*op. cit.*, p. 393) and Miss Norgate (*John Lackland*, p. 84) pass over in silence the reasons given in the sentence, as our chronicler relates them. As for M. Guilhiermoz (*Bibl. de l'Ec. des Chartes*, 1899, pp. 48, 65), he makes very free with the text of Ralph of Coggeshall, which he interprets in the most arbitrary manner.

Breton, and the Pope himself. The testimony of Ralph of
Coggeshall cannot prevail against their silence. Innocent
III., to whom it was Philip Augustus's strong interest
to give information respecting the trial and three
chroniclers well situated for hearing it spoken of were
ignorant of the condemnation; consequently it never
occurred.

The very first reading of this argument reveals one
of its weak points; Miss Norgate's scepticism is highly
Exaggerated exaggerated, it is "hypercriticism." If we
scepticism had to reject all the historical facts which
are only known to us from one source, a great part of
our knowledge of the past would crumble away. And
Miss Norgate would be obliged to suppress many pages
of her works, notably of her *John Lackland,* where she
often confides in the unsupported testimony of the
biographer who wrote the metrical life of William the
Marshal. Given the weakness of historical science and
the mediocrity of the materials at its disposal, it is
necessary to admit information derived from a single
document, on the double condition that the general
veracity of that document has been tested on other points,
and that on the particular point in question it is not in
contradiction with our other sources.

Now this twofold condition is fulfilled as far as
concerns the testimony of Ralph of Coggeshall. His
                    chronicle is indisputably one of the most
Great value of precise and most exact that we have for the
the evidence of
Coggeshall first twenty-five years of the thirteenth
                    century. On the other hand, Rigord,
Guillaume le Breton and Gervase of Canterbury, whose
narrative, be it remarked, is much briefer than Ralph's,
say nothing which forbids us to accept the condemnation.
All three state that John failed to appear, and suppressing
mention of the sentence, relate afterwards, like Ralph of
Coggeshall, how Philip Augustus invaded Normandy

and destroyed the castle of Boutavant.[1] It is clear that the details of the trial did not interest them. Just as they do not speak of the dilatory pleas put forward by John, of which Ralph of Coggeshall informs us,[2] they have omitted to relate that a condemnation by default had been pronounced; was not this condemnation a matter of course, and why should the court of Philip Augustus have abstained from passing this sentence the necessity of which was self-evident? The event was so natural that there was hardly need to describe it.

As for the letter addressed by Innocent III. to John Lackland on the 31st of October, 1203, a year and a half after these events and seven months after the death of Arthur, it appears to us not only to be reconcilable with the statements of Ralph of Coggeshall, but to absolutely corroborate them, and this document, in which Miss Norgate seeks her most decisive arguments, appears to be the one which definitively rebuts her thesis.

Innocent III's letter proves it

In this celebrated letter,[3] the Pope communicates to the king of England the reasons which Philip Augustus has placed before the Holy See, "per suas literas et nuntios," to justify his conduct. Evidently, Innocent III., being impartial, must have faithfully reproduced these reasons. Now the justification put forward by the king of France, as the Pope summarizes it, confirms the narrative of Ralph de Coggeshall almost word for word, even on the precise point under discussion in Miss Norgate's article;

1. This was a castle which John had promised to deliver up as a pledge of his appearance at the court of Philip Augustus; he had refused to fulfil his promise (Guillaume le Breton, ed Delaborde, i, pp. 207, 209, 210). The destruction of the castle of Boutavant was therefore a logical consequence of the condemnation; and we may even say that it implies it. Ralph of Coggeshall says with the precision which distinguishes his whole narrative : " Hoc igitur curiae suae judicium rex Philippus gratanter acceptans et approbans, coadunato exercitu, confestim invasit castellum Butavant " (Ed. Stevenson, p. 136).

2. Guillaume le Breton gives them only a single word, "post multos defectus."

3. Potthast, *Regesta Pontificorum Romanorum*, No. 2013. Miss Norgate dates it by mistake the 29th October.

and it is curious that that scholar was not struck by the singular agreement of the two documents. In both we see that it is on an appeal of vassals that Philip Augustus acted; that he first repeatedly required King John to make peace with his vassals; that, not being able to get any satisfaction, he cited him before his court, with his barons' concurrence. From this point the two narratives differ somewhat; Ralph of Coggeshall insists on the privilege alleged by the King of England, who claimed to have the right not to appear at Paris, while Philip Augustus, in the letter summarized by Innocent III., insists on his attempts at accommodation. But Miss Norgate failed to see, and I do not know whether anybody has yet observed, that the bull of Innocent III. contains a clear allusion to the condemnation : *Although the king of France,* writes the Pope, *had defied you (diffidasset) by the counsel of his barons and his men* and war had broken out, he sent you again four of his knights, charged to ascertain whether you were willing to repair the wrongs committed towards him, and to cause you to know that in the contrary case he would henceforth conclude alliance against you with your men, wherever he could. And you have

The "defiance" proves previous sentence

avoided those who sought you. . . ." The term *diffidare* has here evidently its full and formal sense : it is the solemn rupture of the feudal relationship; now, as M. Luchaire says in his *Manuel d'Institutions,*[1] " defiance can only take place between suzerain and vassal after the suzerain has summoned his feudatory to appear before his court and *has had him condemned there,* either present or by default." The moment that Philip declares he has defied John Lackland there is proof that the court has previously given its sentence.[2]

1. *Manuel d'Institutions françaises* (1892), p. 230.
2. The pope adds that Philip Augustus acknowledges having, after these events, received the homage of certain vassals of the king of England, "quod *contumaciae tuae* asserit imputandum."

H

It is not surprising that Philip Augustus did not give the Pope circumstantial details respecting the condemnation by default and the text of the sentence. It was not his interest to do this **The letter to the Norman bishops** in a letter in which he strove above everything to convince the Pope of his conciliatory spirit; and he contented himself therefore with telling the Pope that by the counsel of his barons and his men, *de baronum et hominum suorum consilio,* he had broken the feudal tie which bound him to John, *diffidasset.* This is why, in his letter of the 7th of March, 1205, to the Norman bishops[1] a letter on which Miss Norgate has no right to found an argument, Innocent III., ill-informed upon the trial of 1202, maintains an attitude of reserve. Philip Augustus is requiring the bishops to swear fealty to him because he has acquired Normandy upon a sentence of his court: *asserens quod, justitia praeeunte, per sententiam curiae suae Normanniam acquisivit;* the Pope, consulted by the bishops as to what they ought to do, cannot give them an answer in default of sufficient information : *quia vero nec de jure, nec de consuetudine nobis constat, utpote qui causam, modum et ordinem, aliasque circumstantias ignoramus.* He does not say that he has never heard of this condemnation of 1202; but he is ignorant of its precise tenour and the circumstances, and he is not well acquainted with the custom of France.

The letter of the 31st October, 1203, is in short the most important text which we possess for the solution of the problem of the two trials of John Lackland. By the absolute silence it maintains respecting the death of Arthur it proves convincingly that seven months after John's alleged condemnation by the peers of France as the murderer of his nephew, nothing was known at Rome either of the death of the young prince or of the

1, Potthast, *op cit.*, No. 2434.

condemnation which was its supposed consequence. By *Bémont's contrary* the summary which it gives of the apology which the *conclusion is* King of France had made for his conduct, it confirms *correct,* the assertions of the very exact Ralph de Coggeshall.

M. Bémont's conclusions then still hold the field. John Lackland was not condemned to death by the court of France as murderer of Arthur in 1203,

M. Bémont's conclusions hold their ground

but he was condemned in 1202 by default, to the loss of his French fief, for disobedience and refusal of service to his suzerain.

The appeal of the Poitevin barons, a fine opportunity for preparing annexations, eagerly seized by Philip Augustus, was thus the indirect cause of the

Constitutional importance of the question

separation of Normandy and England; an event of immense importance for the English constitution as well as for French policy; for the monarchy of the Plantagenets was suddenly detached from a province from which it had derived a part of its institutions and its administrative staff, and, on the other hand, as Stubbs says, " the king found himself face to face with the English people."

XI.

AN " UNKNOWN CHARTER OF LIBERTIES."

Round's "Unknown Charter of Liberties" is the report of an agent of Philip Augustus.
— H. W. C. Davis.

THERE exists in our *Trésor des Chartes* a list of " concessions of King John " to his barons, which was printed as early as 1863 by Teulet, in his *Layettes*.[1] This document had completely escaped scholars working upon English history until the moment at which it was " discovered " by Mr. Round in a copy forming part of the *Rymer Transcripts*, and published by him in the *English Historical Review*.[2] It is celebrated now under the name, inaccurate it will be seen, which Mr. Round has given to it of the " Unknown Charter of Liberties." As this so-called " Unknown Charter of English Liberties," certainly interesting, has only been studied since 1893, as Stubbs does not quote a single line of it, as he did not insert it in the last edition of his *Select Charters*, and as it is not to be found correctly transcribed in any of the books which French libraries usually possess, we reproduce it here.[3]

History of "unknown charter"

The manuscript, the writing of which is French and dates from the first quarter of the thirteenth century, contains, first, a copy of the charter of Henry I., preceded by these words: "Charta quam Henricus, communi baronum consilio rex coronatus, eisdem et prelatis regni Angliae

Copy of the charter of Henry I

1. *Layettes du Trésor des Chartes*, publ. par A. Teulet, i, 1863, p. 423.

2. J. H. Round, *An unknown Charter of Liberties, English Histor. Review*, viii, 1893, pp. 288 sqq.

3. We shall follow the text given by Mr. MacKechnie, *Magna Carta*, pp. 569–570.

plurima privilegia concedit," and followed by the note:
" Hec est carta regis Henrici per quam barones querunt
libertates, et hec consequentia concedit rex Johannes.[1]

Next follows the list of the " concessions of King
Text of the John," here given; we shall indicate for
document each clause [2] the analogous clauses of the
charter of Henry I.,[3] of the *Articuli Baronum* (June,
1215) [4] and of the Great Charter:[5]

1. " Concedit rex Johannes quod non capiet hominem
absque judicio, nec aliquid accipiet pro justitia, nec
injustitiam faciet " (Cf. *Articles of the Barons*, art. 29
and 30; *Great Charter*, art. 39 and 40.[6])

2. " Et si contingat quod meus baro vel homo meus
moriatur et heres suus sit in etate, terram suam debeo
ei reddere per rectum releveium absque magis capiendi."
(Cf. *Charter of Henry I.*, 2; *Articles of the Barons*, 1;
Great Charter, 2.)

3. " Et si ita sit quod heres sit infra etatem, debeo
quatuor militibus de legalioribus feodi terram bajulare
in custodia, et illi cum meo famulo debent mihi reddere
exitus terre sine venditione nemorum et sine redemptione
hominum et sine destructione parci et vivarii; et tunc
quando ille heres erit in etate, terram ei reddam quietam."
(Cf. *Articles of the Barons*, 2—3; *Charter*, 3—4.)

4. " Si femina sit heres terre, debeo eam maritare,
consilio generis sui, ita non sit disparagiata. Et si una
vice eam dedero, amplius eam dare non possum, sed se

1. Round, *loc. cit.*, p. 288, and H. Hall, quoting a letter of M.
Bémont, in *English Histor. Review*, ix, 1894, p. 327.

2. The division into clauses does not exist in the original any more
than it does in the Great Charter.

3. Liebermann, *Gesetze*, i, pp. 521 sqq., or Bémont, *Chartes des
libertés anglaises*, pp. 3 sqq.

4. Bémont, pp. 15 sqq. The true title is: *Capitula que barones petunt
et dominus rex concedit.*

5. Bémont, pp. 26 sqq.

6. Cf. also the letter patent of the 10th of May, 1215, in Rymer, Rec.
edition, i, p. 128, and the excellent commentary which Mr. MacKechnie
gives on article 39 of the Great Charter (*Magna Carta*, pp. 436 sqq.).

maritabit ad libitum suum, sed non inimicis meis." (Cf. *Henry I.*, 3; *Articles*, 3 and 17; *Charter*, 6 and 8.)

5. " Si contingat quod baro aut homo meus moriatur, concedo ut pecunia sua dividatur sicut ipse diviserit; et si preoccupatus fuerit aut armis aut infirmitate improvisa, uxor ejus, aut liberi, aut parentes et amici propinquiores, pro ejus anima, dividant." (Cf. *Henry I.*, 7; *Articles*, 15—16; *Charter*, 26—27.)

6. " Et uxor ejus non abibit de hospitio infra XL dies et donec dotem suam decenter habuerit, et maritagium habebit." (Cf. *Henry I.*, 4; *Articles*, 4; *Charter*, 7.)

7. "Adhuc hominibus meis concedo ne eant in exercitu extra Anglia nisi in Normanniam et in Britanniam et hoc decenter; quod si aliquis debet inde servitium decem militum, consilio baronum meorum alleviabitur."

8. " Et si scutagium evenerit in terra, una marca argenti capietur de feodo militis; et si gravamen[1] exercitus contigerit, amplius caperetur consilio baronum regni." (Cf. *Articles*, 32; *Charter*, 12.)

9. "Adhuc concedo ut omnes forestas quas pater meus et frater meus et ego afforestavimus, deafforesto." (Cf. *Henry I.*, 10; *Articles*, 47; *Charter*, 47, 53.)

10. "Adhuc concedo ut milites qui in antiquis forestis meis suum nemus habent, habeant nemus amodo ad herbergagia sua et ad ardendum; et habeant foresterium suum; et ego tantum modo unum qui servet pecudes meas." (Cf. *Articles*, 39; *Charter*, 47.)

11. " Et si aliquis hominum meorum moriatur qui Judeis debeat, debitum non usurabit quamdiu heres ejus sit infra etatem." (Cf. *Articles*, 34; *Charter*, 10.)

12. " Et concedo ne homo perdat pro pecude vitam neque membra." (Cf. *Articles*, 39; *Charter*, 47; *Charter of the Forest*, of 1217, article 10.)

What is this document? What is its origin, what does it represent?

---

1. Mr. Hubert Hall, *loc. cit.*, p. 329, proposes the correction : allevamen.

None of the numerous hypotheses formulated so far by English scholars quite satisfies us. We must put **Different** aside to begin with, as untenable, the idea **suppositions** of a charter granted by John, in 1213, to the barons of the North, to the " Norois,"[1] and the supposition of a forged coronation charter of John Lackland, fabricated in 1216—1217 to legitimize the pretensions of Lewis of France.[2]

Mr. Prothero's theory is less unacceptable; it is that it was a charter of liberties offered by the king to the baronage, in the first four months of the year 1215, in order to calm the discontent and uneasiness of the nobles, in the same way that he had wished to appease the clergy by granting them liberty of election.[3]

Mr. Prothero remarks with reason that this list of concessions interests almost exclusively the nobility. But, even admitting that the form of the document authorises this supposition, it would be very singular that no chronicler should have made any allusion to so important an offer; very singular that the nobility should have rejected it; very singular, finally, that John should have spontaneously offered never to require the military service of the English knights, for his expeditions in the centre and south of France, seeing that this weighty concession is not mentioned in the Great Charter itself. Mr. MacKechnie makes the converse supposition; that we have here not an offer of the king, but a preparatory schedule proposed by the barons in the month of April, 1215, and mentioned moreover by Roger of Wendover.[4]

But Roger of Wendover says that this schedule was

1. This is the explanation proposed, with all reserves, by Mr. Round, *English Historical Review*, viii, 1893, pp. 292 sqq. See the decisive objections of Mr. Prothero, *ibidem*, ix, 1894, pp. 118 sqq.

2. See the article by Mr. Hubert Hall, *ibidem*, ix, 1894, pp. 326 sqq.

3. Prothero, *Note on an unknown Charter of Liberties*, *ibidem*, ix, 1894, p. 120.

4. MacKechnie, *Magna Carta*, p. 204.

rejected by the king,[1] and our text runs: "hec consequentia *concedit* rex Johannes."

In these explanations, too, no account is taken of the singularly clumsy form which this document assumes.

Neither an authentic nor an apocryphal charter We have seen that it commences thus: "concedit rex Johannes quod . . . ," and that in the following sentence the king begins to speak, expressing himself in the first person: he even expresses himself in the first person singular, contrary to the usage of John Lackland's chancery. If we had to do with a charter offered by the king, or a document proposed by the barons, or even with a forged charter fabricated by the French, these anomalies would not present themselves.

We believe, therefore, with Mr. H. W. C. Davis, who has quite recently studied the problem afresh,[2] that the so-called "unknown charter," is not a **It is a report** charter, but an informal report of the negotiations which ended in the drawing up of the Great Charter. By whom was it drawn up and at what exact moment? We will not say with Mr. Davis, that the author, having transcribed the charter of Henry I. with so pious a respect was evidently a partisan of the barons; that his Latin betrays an English rather than a French origin;[3] that the composition of article 12 reveals the humbleness of his rank;[4] nor that the document must have been drawn up during the three

1. "Affirmavit tandem cum juramento furibundus, quod nunquam tales illis concederet libertates, unde ipse efficeretur servus" (Wendover, in Matt. Paris, *Chron. Maj.;* ed. Luard (Rolls series), ii, p. 586).

2. In the *English Historical Review,* xx, 1905, pp. 719 sqq.

3. Mr. Hubert Hall, *loc. cit.*, p. 333, on the contrary, points out "Gallicisms" in it. These hypotheses seem to me very unprofitable.

4. The author, according to Mr. Davis, declaims in literary rather than legal phrase, against the Forest Law, so hard upon poor people. Mr. Davis does not notice that: (1) The Forest Law also greatly injured the interests of the barons; (2) The Charter of the Forest, of 1217, contains an article drawn up in very similar terms (Art. 10 in Bémont, p. 67): "Nullus de cetero amittat vitam vel membra pro venacione nostra."

days[1] which passed between the acceptance of the *Articuli Baronum* and the publication of the Great Charter. To us it seems possible to affirm this, and this only :

1. The document is in close relation with the *Articuli Baronum* and the Great Charter. Only the article relative to the service in the host abroad and two complementary clauses touching the Forest, have no equivalent in the *Articuli Baronum,* or the Charter.

2. Our document is not an official text. It is a memorandum, it is notes taken by a spectator. He is well informed; he is struck by the importance attached by the barons to the charter of Henry I., to the extent of transcribing that charter entire at the beginning of his minute; he reports certain of the king's concessions almost in the terms in which they were officially drafted. But he is neither a jurist, for his diction is at times very loose,[2] nor a personage directly interested in the concessions made, for he often does not understand the sense of them and distorts them in the summary he gives of them.[3]

1. MacKechnie, *Magna Carta,* p. 45, has proved that the *Articuli Baronum* were accepted by the king and sealed with his seal on the 15th of June (the date borne by the Great Charter itself) and that the Great Charter was sealed and published on the 19th.

2. Cf. the inexact drafting of article 1; the *cum meo famulo* of article 3, etc.

3. Clause 1 is a vague and inaccurate summary of the pretensions so clearly formulated in the *Articles of the Barons* and the *Great Charter.* One would not suspect, in reading it, that what the barons really wished for was a return to feudal justice, as it existed before the great legal and judicial revolution of the reign of Henry II. In article 5 the demands of the barons as regards inheritances have not been well understood; the main object was to prevent the king's servants from carrying out wrongful seizures; the true sense of clauses 26–27 of the Great Charter does not appear here. Similarly, in article 11, the author of our document did not perhaps understand that the barons, as far as concerns debts to the Jews, chiefly wished to protect themselves against the greed of the king. Mr. Hubert Hall (see above, p. 118, note 1) thinks that in article 8 the scribe has replaced *allevamen* by *gravamen;* in our opinion it is not a question of an error of transcription; the French agent, who, let us believe, was the author of the document, must have supposed that scutage was a simple tax in substitution for military service, such as existed in France for the " roturiers " in the

3. Our document exists in the original in the *Trésor des Chartes,* in which our kings preserved the records which directly interested the Crown of France, its rights and its designs. The handwriting is French, and there is no strong reason for believing that the compiler was an Englishman. Still, as Mr. Davis has recognised, he might have been an Englishman in the service of the king of France.

The work of an agent of Philip Augustus

However this may be, it appears to us beyond question that the manuscript has been shut up in the *layettes* of the *Trésor* since the times of Philip Augustus. That prince, as we know, had agencies on the other side of the Channel; he offered succour to the rebel barons, sent the pirate Eustace the Monk to convey to them war machines, and this attitude helped to bring about the concession of the Great Charter.[1]

Evidently he had confidential agents who kept him informed respecting the negotiations taking place between John Lackland and his barons. The alleged "unknown charter of English Liberties" is the report of an agent of Philip Augustus.

4. The very character of our document forbids us to assign a precise date to it. We can only say that it is a little anterior to the *Articuli Baronum,* and dates from a moment at which the agreement between the king and the barons already appears as certain, without being definite. Everything inclines us to believe that negotiations were entered upon before the Runnymede interview, and we have before us an account of these negotiations, at a moment when the rumour ran that such and such

time of Philip Augustus (see Borrelli de Serres, *Recherches sur divers services publics,* i, 1895, pp. 467 sqq.) and that the tax became heavier if the service in the host required was more exacting. *Allevamen exercitus,* proposed by Mr. Hubert Hall, would make the meaning as follows : If there is exemption from service the tax to pay on this count (and to add to the scutage) shall be determined upon the advice of the barons.

1. See my *Etude sur la vie et le règne de Louis VIII,* p. 69.

concessions had been granted by the king. If Philip Augustus' agent had written after the publication of the *Articuli Baronum* or of the Great Charter, he would have contented himself with sending into France a copy of the official text.

Is this as much as to say that the "unknown charter" has no historical interest? Far from it. It is a new proof of the curiosity with which events in **Interest of the** England were followed in France; a new **document** proof also of the part played by the spirit of tradition and of the prestige exercised by the charter of Henry I. In addition, it contains a clause which does not occur either in the *Articles of the Barons* or in the *Great Charter,* and clauses which are only to be found there in a very altered form; in this way it enlightens us respecting the hesitations and mutual concessions of the two parties, and explains better why the barons gave this or that form to certain of their claims. This is what the scholars who have studied it up till now have not sufficiently observed.

The clauses on the repression of judicial abuses committed by the king (article 1), on the amount of the feudal relief (article 2), on the right of wardship (article 3), on the debts of minors to the Jews (article 11), on the marriage of heiresses (article 4), on dowry and the dower of widows (article 6), on the disposal of pecuniary inheritances after the decease of the testator or intestate person (article 5), are to be found again, in a more technical and generally a more complete form, in the Great Charter.[1] Some of them resemble more the *Articuli Baronum,* others the definitive charter. There is no need to insist at length on the details of the wording, as the differences may depend on the varying care and success with which the author of our document has summarized what he intended to report, and, I repeat, he

1. On the subject of clause 5, see Miss Mary Bateson, *Borough Customs*, ii, 1906, p. cxliii.

appears not to have always understood the exact sense of the clauses which he noted.

What is more interesting is this; articles 9, 10, and 12 touching the Royal forest, give us light upon the concessions which the barons had at first intended to wrest from the king.[1] According to clause 9, John would appear to have engaged to disafforest the forests created by himself, by Richard, and by Henry II. In clause 47 of the *Articuli Baronum* and of the Great Charter, it is only the forests created in the reign of John that are to be disafforested. Article 53 of the Charter proves however that the king had pledged himself to enquire whether certain forests of Richard and Henry II. ought not to be disafforested; our document is useful therefore for the understanding of article 53 of the Great Charter. Articles 10 and 12 of our document establish that the knights who possess a wood in the royal forests of ancient date, may henceforth cut trees and branches there for building and fuel; they shall have in their wood a forester in their service, and the king can only place a single forester there, for the purpose of protecting the game. According to article 12, no one may be condemned to death or to mutilation, for an offence touching the royal game. Important as were these concessions, the barons were not content with them; they preferred, in clause 39 of the Articuli and clause 48 of the Great Charter, to demand the constitution of elective juries in each county, to make enquiry concerning all the " evil customs " of the royal forests. The " evil customs " denounced by these juries of

Articles touching the Forest

1. Stubbs (i, p. 434 sqq.) has explained what the Royal Forest was and how it was administered. Cf. G. J. Turner, Preface to the *Select pleas of the Forest* (1901) and the good summary of MacKechnie, *Magna Carta*, pp. 482 sqq. This irritating question of the Forest interested the baronage as well as the popular classes. It was the people of small consequence who suffered most from the abuse of power of the royal foresters; but the barons who had lands comprised within the forest bounds also submitted with impatience to the prohibitions of every kind issued to protect the trees and game.

inquest were to be immediately abolished; a plan very
dangerous to the royal authority, and which would have
ended in the complete suppression of a prerogative to
which the Norman and Angevin kings attached the
highest value.   As a matter of fact, the civil war
prevented these juries from completing their work.   The
council of regency of Henry III., in 1217, granted a
Forest Charter : in article 10, the penalty of death and
mutilation is abolished for poaching offences.   We see
that as early as 1215 the barons had demanded the
abolition of these cruel penalties.

According to articles 7 and 8 of our document, the
men of the king do not owe military service outside
England, except in Normandy and in
Brittany, and even then under certain
conditions (*et hoc decenter*); if any one
owes the service of ten knights, the assembly of the
barons will grant him an "alleviation."[1]   If the king
levies a scutage, he will only take a mark of silver from
each knight's fee.[2]

Foreign service
and scutage

These clauses are very interesting.   All that is said in
the *Articuli Baronum* (art. 32) and in the *Great Charter*
(art. 12) is that, beyond the aid in the three cases, no
scutage can be levied without the consent of the
Commune Consilium regni, and they were contented
with specifying that the rate should be "reasonable."
At the time to which our document belongs, we see that
the barons did not think of preventing the king from
freely levying the scutage of one mark.   On the other
hand, it seems that, by means of mutual concessions,

1. That is to say, according to Mr. Hall's interpretation (*loc. cit.*,
p. 327), instead of furnishing knights he will pay a composition.

2. The text adds : if there is an increase of military obligations, a
higher scutage may be collected, but on the counsel of the barons of
the realm. As we have said above (p. 121, n. 3), there must be a
mistake here. Scutage was not a mere tax for providing substitutes as
Stubbs tended to believe; at any rate, in the reign of John, it was an
addition to the effective military service, and did not exempt from it.
See above, p. 56, note 1, a note on scutage.

they had come to an agreement with the king for the settlement of the troublesome question of military service in France; they agreed to accompany him in the provinces bordering on the Channel, but not beyond. Why is any clause of this kind wanting in the *Articuli Baronum* and the Great Charter? We may conjecture that neither the king nor the barons cared to make engagements on this head and to maintain the ephemeral concessions the memory of which is preserved in the notes we have just analysed.

Such is the supposed "unknown charter of English liberties." It will be observed that there is no question either of the clergy or the merchants, or the towns, and that the royal concessions it contains are made entirely or almost entirely to the nobility. Was it because in the eyes of the French agent who drew up these notes, the negotiations between the king and the barons concerned very specially the particular interests of the latter? And, if this hypothesis is correct, was the French agent wrong? That is a question we shall now have to discuss.

Almost all these concessions relate to the nobility alone

XII.

THE GREAT CHARTER.

Importance of the Great Charter

It will be well to describe here the ideas which appear to prevail to-day, in regard to the constitutional importance of the Great Charter; they are not at all in agreement with the classical, " orthodox " exposition of Stubbs.

According to Stubbs it is the work of the nation

The bishop of Oxford considers that the Great Charter is the work of the whole nation, joined in a coalition against the king : " The demands of the barons," he cries in an almost lyrical tone, "were no selfish exaction of privilege for themselves. . . . . They maintain and secure the right of the whole people as against themselves as well as against their master; clause by clause, the rights of the commons are provided for as well as the rights of the nobles. . . . . The Great Charter is the first great public act of the nation after it has realised its own identity." The 12th and following articles, concerning the levy of scutages and aids and the summons of the *Magnum Concilium* are "those to which the greatest constitutional interest belongs; for they admit the right of the nation to ordain taxation." [1]

Hallam,[2] Gneist,[3] Green,[4] M. Glasson,[5] Boutmy,[6]

1. Stubbs. *Const. Hist.*, i, 570, 571, 573, 579. Cf. Stubbs' preface to the *Historical Collections of Walter of Coventry* (Rolls series), ii, p. lxxi sqq.

2. *Middle Ages*, ii, 447; quoted by MacKechnie, *Magna Carta*, p. 134.

3. *History of Engl. Parliament;* English translation by A. H. Keane, 4th edition, 1895, p. 103.

4. *Short History of the English People*, illus. ed., i, 240 sqq.

5. *Hist. du droit et des instit. de l'Angleterre*, iii, 1882, p. 6.

6. *Développement de la Constitution de la Soc. politique en Angleterre*, 1887. p. 55., and English Translation by I. M. Eaden (*The English Constitution*, 1891), p. 29.

also regard the Great Charter as a constitutional victory gained by the nation as a whole over the king. The majority of English historians of the 19th century exalted the Great Charter with the same fervour, and the "sentimental force" which the course of historical events has given to this contract between King John, the English Church, and the *liberi homines* of the kingdom is not yet exhausted.

Texts have to be read, however, without preoccupying ourselves with the importance which has been attributed to them in later ages, and if we apply a like **Reaction in** method to the study of the Great Charter, **modern criticism** we form a very different judgment upon it. Without claiming to have been the initiator of this reaction,[1] I may be allowed to recall, that, in a work published in 1894, I drew very different conclusions from the study of the sources used by Stubbs and also of documents which he had not utilised, and that I wrote as follows : " The barons had no suspicion that they would one day be called the founders of English liberty. The patriotism of writers on the other side of the Channel has singularly misrepresented the nature of this crisis. They extol the *noble simplicity* with which the people asserted its rights. But the authors of the Great Charter had no theories or general ideas at all. They were guided by a crowd of small and very practical motives in extorting this form of security from John Lackland."[2]

A decade ago the Great Charter underwent in England itself a critical examination which was not favourable to it. In their admirable *History of English Law* of which

1. Hallam said : "It has been lately the fashion to depreciate the value of Magna Carta, as if it had sprung from the private ambition of a few selfish barons, and redressed only some feudal abuses". (quoted by MacKechnie, *Magna Carta*, p. 134). I do not know what authors are alluded to in this passage, and there is no use in trying to find out. In any case this " depreciation " is excessive. The Great Charter did not do nothing but "redress some feudal abuses." As we shall see, it struck at all the abuses of the royal power, from which the nobility had to suffer, directly or indirectly.

2. *Etude sur la vie et le règne de Louis VIII.* pp. 57–58.

the first edition appeared in 1895, Sir Frederick Pollock *it is a ecclesias-*
and Mr. Maitland observe very justly that it contains *tical + baronial*
almost no novelty. It is essentially a conservative or *reaction against*
even reactionary document. Its most salient charac- *the increasing power*
teristic is the restoration of the old feudal *of the crown.*

Conservative and reactionary character of the Great Charter law, violated by John Lackland, and perhaps its practically most important clauses, because they could be really *it seeks to restore the old feudal rights of the barons, etc.*
applied, were, that for example which
limited the right of relief, or that which forbad the king
to keep the land of a felon for more than a year and a
day, to the detriment of the lord. Upon other points,
the Great Charter marks an ecclesiastical and aristocratic
reaction against the growth of the crown.[1] Sir
Frederick Pollock and Mr. Maitland express this opinion
with discretion, and without denying the high value of
the Great Charter. Another jurist, Mr. Edward Jenks,
has shown less reserve : he sees in the movement of 1215
nothing but an attempt at a feudal reaction, and showers
the bolts of his iconoclastic zeal on the "myth of the
Great Charter." [2]

Miss Kate Norgate in her *John Lackland*, gives only
a brief and superficial analysis of the Great Charter.
But at least she shows very clearly that the
Political incapacity of the Baronage authors of this "peace" were, not the body
of the English baronage, but to use the
evidently very exact words of Ralph of
Coggeshall, " the archbishop of Canterbury, several
bishops and some barons." The attitude of the barons
before the crisis of 1215 and after the conclusion of the
pact of Runnymede, proves clearly, she says, that the
mass of the baronage were incapable of rising to the

1. Pollock and Maitland, *History of English Law,* 2nd edition, 1898,
i, pp. 171 sqq. See also MacKechnie, *op. cit.*; this careful commentator
has shown that as a whole the Great Charter restores custom; by that
very fact, it is at times reactionary; on some points only, it marks a
step in advance.

2. *The Myth of Magna Carta* in the *Independent Review*, Nov., 1904.

I

conception of a contract between the king and all the free classes of the nation. Before the crisis of 1215, the barons had let John persecute the Church without doing anything to defend it; after the signature of the Charter, these pretended champions of Right did not even know how to respect their plighted faith.[1] Mr. Pollard, in his *Henry VIII.*, has developed an analogous idea: vigorously and thoroughly enquiring why the Tudors were able to reign despotically, he finds only one possible explanation. We must renounce that idea —an idea so dear to Stubbs—that for seven hundred years England has been the messenger of liberty in the world. The English were but men and, in a general way, " the English ideal was closely subordinated to the passion for material prosperity," and not to the love of liberty for its own sake. That the English have always burned with enthusiasm for parliamentary government, is a legend invented by modern doctrinaires. The Great Charter, the symbol of this alleged political genius of the Anglo-Saxon race, only became in reality the "palladium of English liberty" in the 17th century, to serve the necessities of the anti-monarchical opposition, and for that purpose it was greatly distorted and travestied. In the 16th century, it did not so to speak come into question, it had been forgotten : Shakespeare does not say a word about it in his " King John." [2]

England has not always been eager for liberty

We are now a long way off from the panegyrics in which the Great Charter is represented as the source of all the greatness and all the political institutions of England, far even from the more measured appreciation of Stubbs. Whatever the respect with which we must regard the work of that eminent scholar, it is clear that, upon the causes of the crisis of

1. *John Lackland* (1902), pp. 219, 234, 236 sqq., and *passim.*
2. A. F. Pollard, *Henry VIII*, ed. in 18mo (1905), p. 33 sqq.

1215, upon the character of the compact, upon the conceptions and the state of mind which engendered it, upon the influence it has had in the development of English liberties, we can no longer profess in all respects the same opinion as he did. Recently a new and learned commentary on the Great Charter has been published[1] of which we shall have to speak again; in reading this work of Mr. MacKechnie, the most thorough and balanced which has been written on the subject, we receive the impression that Stubbs was the dupe of many illusions, and that the historians of his generation have had difficulty in guarding themselves against the legends created by the exaltation of patriotism and by political strife.

It is quite clear that history is written to-day with more sobriety; but we must add that we are better informed respecting the crisis of 1215 than **New light on** they were or could be at the time at which **the subject** the first volume of the *Constitutional History* appeared. In the course of a quarter of a century, English, German, and French scholarship, has thrown much light on most of the questions which are touched on in the Great Charter, and it cannot now be interpreted as it used to be. Moreover, we are enlightened by new documents.

The term " new document " cannot, to speak exactly, be applied to the most important of those of which I am thinking: the *Histoire des ducs de* **Narrative of** *Normandie et des rois d'Angleterre,* **the "Histoire** published in 1840 by Francisque Michel. **des ducs de** **Normandie"** But Stubbs and his contemporaries, who somewhat strangely neglected works of French scholarship, were not acquainted with this chronicle and never utilised it. I believe myself to have been the first to make use of it, at least as far as regards

1. W. S. MacKechnie, *Magna Carta,* 1905.

the history of England.[1] It was written about 1220 by a minstrel attached to Robert of Béthune, who was one of King John's familiars. It is interesting to see how this contemporary summarizes events, and what he recollects of the Great Charter. The barons, he says: "decided to demand of the king that he should observe in regard to them the charters which King Henry, who was his father's grandfather, had granted to their ancestors, and which King Stephen had confirmed to them; and if he refused to do this, they would all throw off their allegiance to him and make war upon him until he was forced to do it. So he had to make such a peace there as the barons wished; there he was forced to agree that a woman should never be married in a quarter where she would be disparaged. This was the best agreement which he made with them, had it been well kept. In addition he had to agree that he would never cause a man to lose member or life for any wild beast that he took; but that he should be able to atone for it by a fine; these two things could readily be tolerated. The reliefs of lands, which were too high, he had to fix at such a rate as they willed to have them. The highest powers of jurisdiction they insisted on having in their lands. Many other things they demanded with much reason, of which I am unable to inform you. Over and above all this they desired that 25 barons should be chosen, and by the judgment of these 25 the king should govern them in all things, and through them redress all the wrongs he should do to them, and they also, on the other hand, would through them redress all the wrongs that they should do to him. Also they further desired, along with all this, that the king should never have power to appoint a bailiff in his land except through the 25. All this the king was forced to concede. For the observance of this peace the king gave his charter to the barons as one who could not help himself."

1. See my *Etude sur la vie et le règne de Louis VIII.*, Introduction, pp. xx–xxi.

It will be convenient to subjoin the original text of the passages here translated :

[Li baron] deviserent que il demanderoient al roi que il lor tenist les chartres que il rois Henris qui fu ayous son père avoit données a lor ancissours et que li rois Estievenes lor avoit confremées ; et se il faire ne le voloit, il le desfieroient tout ensamble, et le guerroieroient tant que il par force le feroit . . . . . Si li couvint là tel pais faire comme li baron vaurrent; là li couvint-il avoir en couvent à force que jamais feme ne marieroit ou liu ù elle fust desparagie. Chou fu la miudre couvenence que il lor fist, s'elle fust bien tenue. O tout chou li couvint-il avoir en couvent ke jamais ne feroit pierdre home menbre ne vie por bieste sauvage k'il presist ;[1] mais raiembre le pooit: ces deus choses pooit-on bien soufrir. Les rachas des tierres, qui trop grant estoient, li couvint metre à tel fuer comme il vaurrent deviser. Toutes hautes justices vaurrent-il avoir en lor tierres. Mainte autre chose lor requisent ù assés ot de raison, que je ne vous sai pas nommer. Desus tout chou vorrent-il que XXV baron fussent esliut, et par le jugement de ces XXV les menast li rois de toutes choses, et toz les tors que il lor feroit lor adreçast par eus, et il autresi de l'autre part li adreceroient toz les tors que il li feroient par eus. Et si vorrent encore avoec tout chou que li rois ne peust jamais metre en sa tierre bailliu, se par les XXV non. Tout chou couvint le roi otriier à force. De cele pais tenir donna li rois sa chartre as barons, comme chil qui amender ne le pot.[2]

In this summary, which is very incomplete, but accurate enough on the whole, the Great Charter appears as a purely feudal compact. What struck

Author's conception of the Great Charter

the minstrel, what evidently struck the men of his time, is that the king, under force and compulsion, had to promise not to disparage heiresses, to diminish the rights of relief, to renounce the strict laws which protected his forests, to respect the rights of justice of the feudal lords, and to recognise the existence of a commission of twenty-five barons, charged to bring to his notice the grievances of the nobility. Not a word of the alleged alliance between the baronage and

[handwritten margin note: The writers of the time regarded as most important the feudal concessions wrung from the King by the barons.]

---

1. This clause does not exist textually in the Great Charter. Cf. above, p. 125.

2. *Histoire des ducs de Normandie*, pp. 145–146, 149–150.

the rest of the nation. The barons are proud, puffed up with their importance, and think only of themselves. "On the strength of this wretched peace they treated him with such pride as must move all the world to pity. They required him to observe quite faithfully what he had agreed with them; *but what they had previously agreed with their men they were unwilling to observe.*"[1]

The biographer of William the Marshal, in the celebrated poem discovered by Paul Meyer, says in two

"History of William the Marshal"
words "That the barons for their franchises came to the king"[2] and afterwards relates at great length the war which followed the annulling of the Great Charter. But he says not a word about the Great Charter itself, does not even quote it.

These are, it is true, chronicles written by minstrels and heralds who are only interested in the doings of the

The "Unknown Charter"
nobles and in feats of arms. But the "unknown charter" which we have recited and commented on above has by no means that character. It is a summary of negotiations between John and his adversaries, the work no doubt of an agent of Philip Augustus, and that king had the greatest interest in knowing the real grounds of the quarrel. Now we have seen that it is concerned almost exclusively with concessions granted to the nobles.

That the Great Charter was drawn up for the baronage and not for the nation as a whole is therefore our

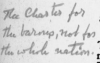

The classical narratives— Wendover, Coggeshall, Barnwell
deduction from documents which Stubbs did not make use of. But it is also the deduction to be drawn from the chronicles which he used, and, lastly, from the Charter itself. Let us read again without preconcep-

1. Avoec toute la vilaine pais, li moustroient-il tel orguel que tous li mons en deust avoir pitié. Il voloient que il moult bien lor tenist chou que en couvent lor avoit; *mais chou que il avoient en covent à lor homes avant ne voloient-il tenir (Ibidem,* p. 151.)

2. Que li baron por lor franchises vindrent al rei . . . *Histoire de Guillaume le Maréchal,* ed. Paul Meyer, *(Soc. de l'Histoire de France,)* ii, pp. 177 sqq.

tion the three principal narratives of the crisis of 1215, those of Roger of Wendover,[1] of Ralph of Coggeshall[2] and of the Canon of Barnwell.[3] We see there that the insurrection is an entirely feudal one; they record only the complicity of the Archbishop of Canterbury and certain bishops and of the " rich men " [4] of London. The insurgents wished " to revive the liberties expressed in the charter of King Henry I.,"[5] which guaranteed the Church and the baronage against a certain number of royal abuses.

These chroniclers speak neither of consent to taxation nor of national union against the king. The Runnymede assembly is composed of "tota Angliae nobilitas regni,"[6] and the Great Charter is a " quasi pax inter regem et barones."[7] The chroniclers are perfectly in agreement with Innocent III., who, in his bull of the 24th August, 1215,[8] speaks of the rebellion of the " magnates et nobiles Angliae," and with John Lackland himself, who calls the crisis the " discordia inter nos et barones nostros," and recognises that he is signing a sort of treaty of peace with his barons.[9]

Let us take the text of the Great Charter, not to recommence clause by clause an analysis already made

1. In the edition of the *Chronica Majora* of Matthew Paris, (Rolls Ser.), ii, pp. 582, 583, 584-589.

2. Ed. Stevenson (Rolls series), pp. 170—173.

3. In the *Historical Collections of Walter of Coventry*, ed. Stubbs (Rolls series), ii, pp. 217—221.

4. " Favebant enim baronibus divites civitatis, et ideo pauperes obmurmurare (or : obloqui) metuebant" (Wendover, p. 587).

5. " Chartam regis Henrici primi proferunt quae libertates exprimit quas proceres, olim abolitas, nunc resuscitare contendunt" (Coggeshall, p. 170).

6. Wendover, p. 589.

7. Coggeshall, p. 172.

8. Printed by (among others) Bémont, *Chartes des Libertés Anglaises*, pp. 41 sqq.

9. "Ad melius sopiendum discordiam inter nos et barones nostros motam" (Great Charter, art. 61; see also art 1). Cf. art. 52 : "in securitate pacis. . . ."

Text of the Great Charter

by Stubbs,[1] but to investigate whether in reality " the barons maintain and secure the rights of the whole people as against themselves as well as against their master," and whether " the rights of the commons are provided for as well as the rights of the nobles," whether, again, the famous articles 12 and 14 " admit the right of the nation to ordain taxation." [2]

Of the sixty-three clauses into which modern editors divide the provisions, often somewhat ill-arranged, of the charter of the 15th of June, 1215,[3] about

Clauses exclusively concerning clergy and nobility

fourteen are temporary articles or relate to the execution of the agreement. Of the forty-nine which remain two concern the clergy,[4] twenty-four specially secure the baronage against the abuse which the king made of his rights as suzerain.[5] These articles, placed for the most

---

1. *Const. Hist.*, i, pp. 572—579. This analysis is in general faithful and exact; but on many points. the interpretation is no longer acceptable. We refer our readers once for all to the excellent commentary by MacKechnie.

2. *Const. Hist.*, i, 570 and 573.

3. We shall quote the Great Charter and the Articles of the Barons (which preceded it and form a sort of first draft of it authentic and approved by the king), from the excellent collection of *Chartes des Libertés Anglaises* of M. Bémont.

4. Arts 1 and 22.

5. Art. 2 to 12, 14 to 16, 21, 26, 27, 29, 32, 34, 37, 39, 43, 46. These articles of feudal law, precise and well drafted, restore ancient custom; two of them, articles 34 and 39, would to some extent have ruined the royal system of justice and the legal progress accomplished since the reign of Henry II, had they been applied in their letter and their spirit, and it is of them above all that we have been thinking in speaking of the reactionary character of the Great Charter : article 34 in fact forbade the king to call up suits touching property, and article 39 restored judgement by peers. They were evidently evoked by the disquieting development of royal justice at the expense of seignorila justice, and by the executions without sentence with which John Lackland had threatened the barons : " Nec super eum ibimus, nec super eum mittemus, nisi per legale judicium parium suorum vel per legem terre." I do not, however, believe that article 39 was drafted with the intention of denying the competence of the professional judges (Cf. article 18 on the iters), and Mr. MacKechnie seems to me to be wrong in seeing in the *lex terre* the old national procedure by battle, compurgation, and ordeal. The *lex terre,* is doubtless the custom of

part at the beginning of the document, are evidently its fundamental clauses in the minds of the authors of the agreement. Ten others concern the general exercise of the royal justice.[1] The benefit of them could not be confined to the barons alone; but it is clear that it was of themselves that the barons were thinking when exacting these guarantees, which, without exception, have for them, directly or indirectly, a powerful interest.[2] It is the same with the important articles which set a limit to the exactions of the sheriffs, to abuses of purveyance, etc. The special régime of the royal Forest was particularly hard on the poor people, but it very much annoyed and irritated the barons themselves.[3]

General clauses against the abuse of royal power

In conclusion, let us take the clauses which appear to be drafted specially in favour of the people of the towns and villages. It is by a study of them that we can verify whether the Great Charter was made " to secure as well the rights of the common people as those of the nobles," and whether " the demands of the barons were no selfish exaction of privilege for themselves."

" Let the city of London," says article 13, " have all its ancient liberties and free customs as well on land

the realm in a general sense, the *lex regni;* cf. the charter granted to the barons on the 10th of May, to settle the same question : " nec super eos per vim vel per arma ibimus, nisi *per legem regni nostri,* etc." (Bémont, p. 33, note).

1. Art : 17, 18, 19, 20, 24, 36, 38, 40, 45, 54.

2. Clause 20, for example, which might seem "democratic," had a financial interest for the lords. See below. Article 17 similarly seems made for the smaller litigants : "Communia placita non sequantur curiam nostram, set teneantur in aliquo loco certo." But this definite fixing of the court of common pleas (that is to say of the suits which did not interest the king personally) at Westminster was not important for the smaller litigants only. The barons might be ruined by the journeys they were until then obliged to make in order to obtain justice. The case of Richard of *Anesty,* who had to follow the king and his court through England, Normandy, Aquitaine and Anjou for five years, is quite characteristic (See MacKechnie, pp. 309–310, and Stubbs, i, 642 and note 1. *Anesty* is Anstey in the county of Hertford; see Round, in *Victoria History of Essex,* i, p. 379.)

3. Clauses 23, 25, 28, 30, 31, 33, 35, 41, 44, 47, 48.

Clauses for the towns as on water." [1] Such is the vague and commonplace concession obtained by the Londoners as the price of their aid. As for the free customs of the other towns, the barons do not even ask, in their *Articuli*, that the king should confirm them. It was only at the time of the definitive drafting of the Great Charter that, perhaps in order to further weaken by generalising the value of the promises made to the Londoners, this phrase was added : " In addition we wish and grant that all the other cities, boroughs, towns and ports may have all their liberties and free customs." It is quite obvious that these " other towns " had taken no active part in the quarrel between the king and the barons, and that they derived no real profit from it.

But the merchants, it will be said, obtain substantial guarantees against arbitrary treatment. By article 20 **Clauses concerning the merchants** they are assured that their merchandise will not be confiscated, under the pretext of fines to be paid. According to article 41, they may go out of, come into and travel in England without paying exhorbitant customs; in article 35 they are promised uniformity of weights and measures. All these concessions were in reality made in the interests of the barons. They saw clearly that the king, by inflicting ruinous fines on the merchants, diminished by so much, to the sole profit of his treasury, the wealth of the lordships to which the condemned men belonged.

---

1. As for the passage relating to the aids paid by the Londoners (see he text and what we have said above pp 101 sqq.) it is very obscure. If this passage means, as some scholars have conjectured, that the aid ought to be *reasonable*, it is too vague to form a guarantee; if it means that every aid levied on the Londoners (except the three feudal aids) must be assented to by the Common Council of the realm, it will be observed that this Common Council, by the terms of article 14, includes only the barons, prelates and tenants-in-chief of the king. It is true that there were 'barons' of London in the Common Council (see Stubbs, p. 398). According to the list given by Matthew Paris (*Chron. Maj.* (Rolls series), ii, pp. 604–605), William Hardel. mayor of London, figures in the Committee of Twenty-five barons elected to keep the king under surveillance in conformity with article 61 of the Great Charter : "quod barones eligant viginti quinque barones de regno quos voluerint."

Article 41, as the context proves, was merely designed to meet the case of the alien merchants who came to visit England to the great convenience of buyers, but were hated and hunted by the native producers. Similarly the uniformity of weights and measures, a reform well calculated to frustrate the frauds of the merchants, was desired by consumers only.

Stubbs wonders that the implements and working beasts of the serf should be exempted from arbitrary fines. But the text reads : ' Et villanus eodem modo amercietur salvo waynagio suo, si inciderint *in misericordiam nostram*.'' What does this engagement made by the king mean ? It means that the "wainage" of a serf prosecuted *before a royal tribunal* shall not be confiscated; only serfs who do not belong to the king and fines imposed by royal officers are in question;[1] the guarantee is given not to the serfs but to the lords; the Charter only concerns itself with these serfs because their "wainage" is the lord's property. It does not protect them against the fines of seignorial courts. Moreover, it does not protect them against arbitrary tallage, and it is clearly specified that the securities relative to royal requisitions are granted only to freemen. Similarly the first article says : " Concessimus *omnibus liberis hominibus* regni nostri omnes libertates subscriptas. . . .'' It might be queried whether the burgesses of the towns are included among the *liberi homines;* it is open to question; but that the serfs or *villani* (we have seen that these are equivalent terms in England in the thirteenth century) were in no wise *liberi homines,* and that by this very fact the great majority of the English population found itself excluded from the benefit of the Great Charter, is a fact which does not admit of doubt.

Clause touching the "wainage" of the villeins

1. This is proved by the slightly different and more precise wording adopted in the confirmations of 1217 and of 1225 : "Villanus alterius quam noster eodem modo amercietur, etc." (Bémont, p. 52). No security is granted to the villeins of the royal demesne; for the rest, their lot was in general better than that of the seignorial villeins.

It is undoubtedly from this standpoint that we must interpret article 60 : " All these aforesaid customs and

Clause concerning the sub-tenants liberties which we have conceded to be observed in our kingdom in our relations with our men (*erga nostros*), all those of our kingdom, as well clerk as lay, shall observe in their relations with their men (*erga suos*)." This clause manifestly does not concern, as Thomson in his commentary thought, the whole of the English people, but only the freemen who did not hold their land directly from the king, and who also wished to be protected against the violence of their lords and the exactions of their agents. In order to understand article 60 we must compare it with article 15, in which the king declares that, just as he will not levy any extraordinary aid on his tenants-in-chief without the consent of the Common Council of the realm, in the same way he will no longer sell any writ authorising a lord to levy an aid on his free tenants (*de liberis hominibus suis*) beyond the three cases recognised by English custom. To sum up, besides the prelates, barons and tenants-in-chief of the king, the only class which obtains precise guarantees is the class of free tenants who are only mediately tenants of the king, and I imagine that this means only the freeholders holding by military service and not simple peasants holding in socage. It was the body of knights, direct and indirect vassals of the king, who had risen against him to obtain " liberties;" it was to them that the barons had made their appeal.[1] It was for them as well as for the barons that the Great Charter was drafted. The Great Charter was essentially a document of feudal law.

This being so, it is very difficult to believe that it contains some new political germ, and institutes the

1. It was probably in 1215 that an appeal was issued of which we have no more than the following mention : " Charta baronum Anglie missa tenentibus Northumbriam, Cumbriam, Westmorlandiam, contra Johannem regem Anglie " (Ayloffe, *Calendar of Ancient Charters*, 1774, p. 328).

The alleged consent to taxation principle of consent to taxation. It is, moreover, the expression and the reflection of a social state in which taxation, properly speaking, is not known. At irregular intervals the king, who is supposed to content himself with the revenues of his demesne for his ordinary necessities, levies an extraordinary tax on some class or other of his subjects; for example, a feudal aid, notably under the form of " scutage," on the knights,—or a carucage on the other freeholders,—or a tallage on the peasants and towns of the crown. Is it said in the Great Charter that whatever may be the form which it takes " taxation " should be assented to? Not in the least. The authors of the compact are not acquainted, let us repeat, **True bearing of the text** with " taxation " in general, and they wish solely to take cognisance of scutage or feudal aids : " That no scutage or aid [1] be established in our kingdom, unless it be to pay our ransom or for the knighting of our eldest son, or for the first marriage of our eldest daughter, and that in these three cases a reasonable aid only be levied." And to please the Londoners these words were added, the obscurity of which we have pointed out : " Let it be the same with regard to the aids of the City of London." Article 14 then specifies the rules for the summons of the Common Council, and, as Stubbs says, evidently does nothing but expressly

---

1. The barons bring together here, as if to confound them, the *auxilium* and the *scutagium*. The *auxilium* is the aid due to the suzerain in virtue of one of the most general principles of feudal law. In France, it is understood that the vassals cannot refuse the *aid in the four cases* : when the suzerain is a prisoner and put to ransom, or when he makes his son a knight, or when he marries his daughter, or when he sets out on the Crusade; in England this last case is not recognised by custom. The *scutagium* in the 12th century was generally a tax levied in lieu of military service, and such is the significance that modern historians, for the most part, give to scutage; but (1) the term might be applied differently, and might have, as early as this period, the general sense of a feudal aid; there are examples of aids in the three cases being called scutage; (2) John Lackland raised scutage which did not dispense from military service (see above, p. 56, note 1, and p. 125). The barons were then justified in assimilating the scutage to the aid.

confirm the previous custom. The king had not the right to levy a feudal aid by his own authority except in the three fixed cases; outside these three cases he had to consult his barons and tenants-in-chief. John Lackland had ignored this usage, or at least he had levied at his discretion, almost every year, a tax, the scutage, to which Henry II. had only resorted seven times and at a more moderate rate. The barons, as the wording of the clause proves, considered scutage as a sort of aid, and the uncertainty of terminology justified them in doing so. In any case the object of article 12 was to remind the king of the custom which regulated the feudal aid in the three cases, and to submit scutage expressly to the same restrictions. When John Lackland had disappeared, this clause was not reproduced in the confirmation of the Great Charter granted on the 12th of November, 1216. We must not conclude from this that the question had no importance in the eyes of the barons, for it was said in article 42 of that confirmation that, upon divers grave and doubtful clauses of the Great Charter, notably on the *levy of scutages and aids,* more ample deliberation was to be taken.[1] It was perhaps the assimilation of the scutage to the feudal aid in the three cases, which was contested by the king's advisers. However this may be, in the confirmations of 1217 and of 1225, clause 12 was replaced by the following one in which no mention is made of the feudal aid in the three cases : "That scutage be henceforth taken as it was accustomed to be taken in the time of King Henry II." [2] This wording clearly proves that the barons had no idea of a parliamentary system, and only wished to be secured, in some way or other, against the too frequent return and the raising of the rate of scutage. Article 14 of the document of 1215, touching

Text adopted in the confirmations

---

1. " Quia vero quedam capitula in priori carta continebantur que gravia et dubitabilia videbantur, scilicet de scutagiis et auxiliis assidendis . . ." (Bémont, p. 58, n. 4).
2. Article 37 (Bémont, p. 57).

the summons of the Common Council is not to be found again in any of the confirmations, and our opinion is that it had been introduced into the Great Charter by desire of the king,[1] and not in the least by desire of the barons. The more so as it does not figure in the *Articles of the Barons.*

The Great Charter of 1215, as we see, was not a political statute, inaugurating constitutional guarantees unknown until then. On the other hand,

The Great Charter is not a national work   far from being a national work, it was manifestly conceived in the interests of a class. What is to be our conclusion? Sir Frederick Pollock and Mr. Maitland, after having pointed out a great number of defects in the Great Charter, add : "And yet with all its faults this document becomes, and rightly becomes, a sacred text, the nearest approach to an irrepealable, ' fundamental statute' that England has ever had. For in brief it means this, that the king is and shall be below the law." [2]   That again, it seems to us, is to assign too glorious a rôle to the baronage of John Lackland and to its political conceptions, which are childish and anarchical. The English nobility of that day has not the idea of law at all. Powerless to prevent the growth of a very strong royal power which has enveloped the country with the network of its administration and its courts, it seeks only to secure itself against financial exactions and the violence of a cruel and tyrannical king. It does not succeed in discovering, and it perhaps does not seek for

1. The end of the clause specifies that "the business should be transacted on the day assigned, by the counsel of those who are present, although all the persons summoned are not come." This is a precaution taken by the king against those who claimed only to pay the tax if they had consented to it in person, and the insertion of this rule is doubtless the principal motive which dictated the insertion of the article. No one, besides, thought that the consecrated usage of the *Common Council* could be abolished and when article 14 disappeared from the confirmations of the Great Charter, assemblies of barons and prelates continued none the less to be convoked.

2. *History of English Law*, i, p. 173.

**Does not
organise the
reign of law**
any " legal " means of controlling his acts and preventing abuses, it does not think of organising the " Common Council," it forgets even to speak of it in the *Articles* which it asks the king to accept. In order to force the king to respect his engagements, what expedient does it devise? The most naïf, the most barbarous procedure,

**Appeal to
civil war**
the procedure of civil war : " The barons shall elect twenty-five barons of the kingdom, who shall with all their power observe, keep and cause to be observed the peace and liberties granted," and in case of need, if the king refuse to repair the wrongs he has committed, " compel and molest him in every way that they can, by taking of his castles, of his lands and of his possessions" with the aid "of the commune of all the land," that is to say, with the aid of all those who are accustomed to bear arms. There is no question, in the Great Charter of John Lackland,[1] of the reign of law; it is merely a question of engagements taken by the king towards his nobles, respect for which is only imposed on him by the perpetual threat of rebellion.

The importance of the Great Charter is in reality due to its fullness, its comprehensiveness, to the variety of

**Reasons of the
constitutional
importance of
the Great
Charter**
the problems which it attempts to solve. It does not differ fundamentally from the charters of liberties which preceded it in the twelfth century, but it is much more explicit. It is five times longer than that of Henry I., it regulates a much greater number of questions, and, being posterior to the capital reforms of Henry II., it is more adapted to the conditions of life and to the state of Law. In passing, and

1. It is quite understood that our remarks cannot apply in their entirety except to the Great Charter of John Lackland. The clause respecting the twenty-five barons has disappeared from the Great Charter of 1225, which has a constitutional importance of the first order, while it is less interesting and less characteristic in the eyes of the historian than that of 1215.

accessorily it enunciates in favour of chartered towns, the merchants and the seignorial villeins, certain promises of which there is no question in the documents conceded at their accession by Henry I., Stephen and Henry II.; although we must reduce the scope of these clauses to its just proportions, the share here assigned to civic liberties is evidently a new and striking fact. Finally, the Great Charter was the result of a celebrated crisis. The aristocracy in arms wrested it by main force from a prince as redoubtable by his intelligence as by his vices, and its publication was followed by a terrible civil war, which ended in its solemn confirmation. It thus became a symbol of successful struggle against royal tyranny; men have discovered in it, in the course of centuries, all sorts of principles of which its authors had not the least notion, and have made of it the " Bible of the Constitution." [1] False interpretations of some of its articles have not been without influence on the development of English liberties. There is no need to seek elsewhere the causes of its success in the Middle Ages and of its long popularity in modern times.

1. Speech of William Pitt, quoted by Bémont, *Chartes*, p. lxix, note 1.

J

INDEX.

MANCHESTER UNIVERSITY PUBLICATIONS.

ANATOMICAL SERIES.

No. I. STUDIES IN ANATOMY from the Anatomical Department of the University of Manchester. Vol. iii. Edited by ALFRED H. YOUNG, M.B. (Edin.), F.R.C.S., Professor of Anatomy. Demy 8vo, pp. ix. 289, 23 plates. 10s. net. (Publication No. 10, 1906.)

"All the papers contained in the volume are real additions to the knowledge of the subject with which they deal. For three of the studies Prof. Young is either in part or wholly responsible, and he is to be congratulated on the vigour shown by the Manchester School of Anatomists."—*Nature*.

"This work affords admirable evidence of the virility of our younger British Universities. It is a notable addition to an already notable series."—*Medical Review*.

"This forms the third volume of the Studies in Anatomy issued by the Council, and contains contributions of considerable interest. The volume is well printed and bound. It speaks well for the activity of investigation at Manchester."—*Lancet*.

"The volume is well got up and is evidence of the continuation of the excellent work which has been carried on for so long a period, under Professor A. H. Young's supervision, and has been encouraged and stimulated by his own work."—*British Medical Journal*.

"Throughout the papers, careful research and accurate observation are manifested, and they will repay careful perusal. To the Anatomist, as well as the practical physician or surgeon, they will prove valuable."
—*Edinburgh Medical Journal*.

CLASSICAL SERIES.

No. I. A STUDY OF THE BACCHAE OF EURIPIDES. By G. NORWOOD, M.A., Assistant Lecturer in Classics. Demy 8vo, pp. xx. 188. 5s. net. (Publication No. 31, 1908.)

"The interest of Mr. Norwood's book, which . . . is a very welcome addition to the bibliography of Euripides, and a scholarly and interesting piece of work, displaying erudition and insight beyond the ordinary, lies in the way in which, by applying Dr. Verrall's methods . . . , he first shows up difficulties and inconsistencies, some of which have hardly been noticed before . . . , and then produces his own startling theory, which he claims is the great solvent of all the perplexities."—*Saturday Review*.

"Unless very strong evidence can be produced against Mr. Norwood's view, it must be accepted as the true solution of the problem. . . . Mr. Norwood is generally clear, and abounds in illuminating thoughts. He has added a full bibliography (running to twenty-three pages) of writings on Euripides, and for this every scholar will offer his sincere thanks. . . . He has done a very good piece of work."—*Athenæum*.

"This volume forms the first of a Classical Series projected by the Manchester University, who are to be congratulated on having begun with a book so original and full of interest. . . . It is admirably argued, and is instinct with a sympathetic imagination. It is, at the very least, an extremely able attempt to solve a very complex problem."
—*Manchester Guardian*.

"Mr. Norwood demonstrates on every page his scholarship and knowledge, and gives proof of much painstaking research. The treatise is as valuable as it is interesting."—*Manchester City News*.

"It is a most ingenious theory, and a reviewer whom it has left unconvinced is all the more bound to give his testimony to the consistent skill, learning, and independence of judgment with which it is presented. The book . . . strikes us as the product of vigorous and independent thought."—*Times*.

MANCHESTER UNIVERSITY PUBLICATIONS.
ECONOMIC SERIES.

No. I.   THE LANCASHIRE COTTON INDUSTRY.   By S. J. CHAPMAN, M.A., M. Com., Stanley Jevons Professor of Political Economy and Dean of the Faculty of Commerce. Demy 8vo, pp. vii. 309.   7s. 6d. net.   (Publication No. 4, 1904.)

" Such a book as this ought to be, and will be, read far beyond the bounds of the trade."—*Manchester Guardian.*

" There have been books dealing with various phases of the subject, but no other has so ably treated it from the economic as well as from the historical point of view."—*Manchester Courier.*

"The story of the evolution of the industry from small and insignificant beginnings up to its present imposing proportions and highly developed and specialised forms, is told in a way to rivet the attention of the reader . . . . . the book is a valuable and instructive treatise on a fascinating yet important subject."—*Cotton Factory Times.*

" Highly valuable to all close students." *Scotsman.*

(GARTSIDE REPORT. No. 1.)

No. II.   COTTON SPINNING AND MANUFACTURING IN THE UNITED STATES OF AMERICA.   By T. W. UTTLEY, B.A., Gartside Scholar.   Demy 8vo, pp. xii. 70.   1s. net.
                                        (Publication No. 8, 1905.)

" Mr. Uttley is to be congratulated on the performance of a not altogether easy task, and his book, in conception and execution, appears to fulfil admirably the intentions of the Trust."—*Manchester Courier.*

" The writer gives ample details concerning wages and other features connected with typical mills . . . and the information thus gathered is of interest and value to the factory operative as well as the student and economist."—*Cotton Factory Times.*

" Mr. Uttley describes how he visited the mills in various States in a very systematic and detailed manner.   Altogether the report makes an admirable and welcome collection of information, and will be found on many occasions worthy of reference."—*Textile Mercury.*

(GARTSIDE REPORT. No. 2.)

No. III.   SOME MODERN CONDITIONS AND RECENT DEVELOPMENTS IN IRON AND STEEL PRODUCTIONS IN AMERICA, being a Report to the Gartside Electors, on the results of a Tour in the U.S.A.   By FRANK POPPLEWELL, B.Sc., Gartside Scholar.   Demy 8vo, pp. vi. 119.   1s. net.
                                        (Publication No. 21. 1906.)

" The American methods of iron and steel production are described, from the practical as well as the statistical side."—*Manchester Courier.*

" Mr. Popplewell writes clearly and well, and he is to be congratulated upon having carried his task through in so entirely a satisfactory manner."—*Manchester City News.*

"America's progress in iron and steel is more wonderful than any bald statistics of production with which we are so familiar can indicate. How that progress has been effected—effected under labour, transport and other difficulties—Mr. Popplewell tells us in an interesting and keenly intelligent review."—*Manchester Guardian.*

"A minute observation of detail . . . characterises the whole work."
                              —*Iron and Coal Trades Review.*

" Mr. Popplewell gives a clear exposition of the results of specialisation in production, of the development of ore-handling machinery, and of the general use of the charging machine, features that characterise American practice.   He shows, too, that the colossal blast-furnace with huge yield due to high-blast pressure, regardless of consumption of steam and boiler coal, is giving place to a blast furnace of more modest dimensions. . . .

MANCHESTER UNIVERSITY PUBLICATIONS.
ECONOMIC SERIES.

"The impression derived from reading Mr. Popplewell's report is that many of the most striking developments, admirable as they are, were designed to meet special wants, and are not necessarily applicable in Great Britain."—*Nature*.

"The book has its interest for the educationist as well as for the manufacturer."—*Scotsman*.

"A chapter of special interest to British consumers is one devoted to the consideration of raw materials."—*Glasgow Herald*.

(GARTSIDE REPORT, No. 3.)

No. IV. ENGINEERING AND INDUSTRIAL CONDITIONS IN THE UNITED STATES. By FRANK FOSTER, M.Sc., Gartside Scholar. Demy 8vo, pp. ix. 106. 1s. net.

(Publication No. 22, 1906.)

"The report under review is of very great interest to those connected with the manufacturing branch of engineering in this country, many of whom will have to relinquish their preconceived notions regarding American methods, if Mr. Foster's conclusions are to be accepted."
—*Electrical Review*.

"The book altogether is very readable, and one we can heartily recommend to all interested in the economics of engineering."
—*The Practical Engineer*.

"Mr. Foster's observation of facts is fresh and interesting . . . . the technical side of his report exhibits much care."—*Manchester Guardian*.

"The book is well worth reading."—*Iron and Coal Trades Review*.

"There is much in the book which will be new to English readers, even to those who have studied the reports of the Moseley and other recent 'commissions.'"—*Belfast News Letter*.

No. V. THE RATING OF LAND VALUES. By J. D. CHORLTON, M.Sc. Demy 8vo, pp. viii. 177. 3s. 6d. net. (Publication No. 23, 1907.)

"A timely and temperate treatise on a subject of growing interest."
—*Pall Mall Gazette*.

"The writer is learned, intelligent, progressive, fair and lucid."
—*Progress*.

"The facts and deductions are well put."—*Western Mail*.

"Chapters upon the scheme of the Royal Commission (minority report) —'Building Land,' 'The Future Increase of Land Values,' 'The Municipal Bill,' and others . . . set forth with clearness and detail some of the many interesting and difficult subjects in connection with valuation, rates and rating."—*Estates Gazette*.

"Mr. Chorlton has made a contribution to this interesting controversy which is worthy of the serious attention of all persons interested in the subject."—*Local Government Chronicle*.

"The arguments for and against this proposed reform in the taxation of land have never been more fairly and freely stated."
—*Liverpool Daily Post and Mercury*.

"Mr. Chorlton deals clearly and concisely with the whole subject of "ating and land values."—*The Standard*.

"The impartiality and candour of Mr. Chorlton's method are beyond dispute, and his book will repay careful study by all who are interested in the question, from whatever motive."—*Westminster Gazette*.

"The first half of this book deserves to become a classic . . . . is one of the best books on a practical economic question that has appeared for many years. It is not only scientifically valuable, but so well written as to be interesting to a novice on the subject."—*The Nation*.

"This thoughtful and judicially expressed treatise."
—*Manchester City News*.

"A very businesslike and serviceable collection of essays and notes on this intricate question."—*Manchester Guardian*.

MANCHESTER UNIVERSITY PUBLICATIONS.
ECONOMIC SERIES.

(GARTSIDE REPORT, No. 4.)

No. VI. DYEING IN GERMANY AND AMERICA. By SYDNEY
H. HIGGINS, M.Sc., Gartside Scholar. Demy 8vo, pp. xiii. 112.
1s. net. (Publication No. 24, 1907.)

" The book will . . . make a valuable addition to the technical literature of this country."—*Tribune.*

" The work is one which . . . . should receive the attention of those
who desire a general view of the German and American dyeing industries."—*Textile Manufacturer.*

"A perusal of the work leads us to the conclusion that much useful
work is being done by the Gartside scholars, which will give these young
men an excellent insight into the working conditions of various
industries."—*Textile Recorder.*

No. VII. THE HOUSING PROBLEM IN ENGLAND. By
ERNEST RITSON DEWSNUP, M.A., Professor of Railway Economics in
the University of Chicago. Demy 8vo, pp. vii. 327. 5s. net.
(Publication No. 25, 1907.)

" Mr. Dewsnup's book is most valuable as it provides all essential information on the subject."—*Standard.*

"All those who are interested in this question, no matter what their
economic predilections, may ponder with advantage Professor Dewsnup's
pages."—*Newcastle Daily Chronicle.*

"The study brings together so weighty an array of facts and arguments that it cannot but prove instructive and suggestive to all classes
of economists interested in its subject."—*Scotsman.*

" Professor Dewsnup's view of the whole problem was stated in 1903,
in a form which won the Warburton Essay Prize at the Manchester
University. Now revised and brought up to date, his valuable work has
taken permanent form."—*Westminster Gazette.*

(GARTSIDE REPORT, No. 5.)

No. VIII. AMERICAN BUSINESS ENTERPRISE. By DOUGLAS
KNOOP, M.A. Price 1s. 6d. net. (Publication No. 30, 1907.)

" The book is calculated to give a clear and accurate description,
" essentially intended for the general reader," and the author has quite
rightly eliminated everything of a technical character, giving his theme
both the simplicity and the interest that are required. . . . The work
might well have been doubled in length without any loss of interest. . . .
Invaluable as a text-book."—*The Economic Journal.*

" Should on no account be missed, for it is a very good attempt at a
survey of the enormous field of American business in the true and
judicial spirit."—*Pall Mall Gazette.*

" Readable, informing, suggestive—full of interest for men engaged in
almost every department of commercial life."—*Manchester City News.*

"A report of the general conditions of industrial work in the United
States, together with a most instructive review of the education of the
business man in their commercial universities."
—*Manchester Daily Dispatch.*

" The report is full of information, and is suggestive throughout."
—*Liverpool Post.*

" Concise, business-like and informative, it emphasises the difference
between the economic positions of England and of America, and cannot
but prove instructive to anyone interested in its subject."—*Scotsman.*

"From the point of view of an intelligent observer and collator,
trained, alert, well-informed, bringing his mind to bear on the fundamental elements of commercial progress and success, it would be
impossible to estimate it too highly."—*Belfast Northern Whig.*

No. IX. THE ARGENTINE AS A MARKET. By N. L. WATSON.
Demy 8vo. 1s. net. (Publication No. 33, 1908.)

MANCHESTER UNIVERSITY PUBLICATIONS

EDUCATIONAL SERIES.

No. I. CONTINUATION SCHOOLS IN ENGLAND & ELSEWHERE. Their place in the Educational System of an Industrial and Commercial State. By MICHAEL E. SADLER, M.A., LL.D., Professor of the History and Administration of Education. Demy 8vo, pp. xxvi 779. 8s. 6d. net. (Publication No. 29, 1907.)

This work is largely based on an enquiry made by past and present Students of the Educational Department of the University of Manchester. Chapters on Continuation Schools in the German Empire, Switzerland, Denmark, and France, have been contributed by other writers.

". . . . gives a record of what the principal nations are doing in the prolongation of school work. It is invaluable as a *corpus* of material from which to estimate the present position of the world—so far as its analogies touch Britain—in 'further education,' as the phrase is."
—*The Outlook.*

"The most comprehensive book on continuation schools that has yet been issued in this country."—*Scottish Review.*

"Professor Sadler has produced an admirable survey of the past history and present condition of the problem of further education of the people . . . . but apart from his own contributions, the bulk of the work, and its most valuable portion, consists of material furnished by teachers and by organisers of schools in various parts of England and Scotland, by officials of the Board of Education and the Board of Trade, and by local education authorities."—*Manchester Guardian.*

"A perfect mine of facts and opinions. . . . is certain of a hearty welcome from all engaged in administering education."—*Glasgow Herald.*

"This is a book which counts. It is a worthy treatment of an all-important subject, and he who wishes his country well must pray that it may be read widely. . . . . I should be glad to think that I have said enough to send many readers post-haste to buy this invaluable treatise."
—L. J. Chiozza Money, M.P., in the *Daily News.*

"Professor Sadler's book is an admirable work on a subject which has not hitherto been dealt with in so masterly and complete a manner."
—*Manchester City News.*

"A volume which may mark a new epoch in educational thought and effort in England."—*The Tribune.*

"This book will for many years remain the standard authority upon its subject."—*The Guardian.*

"It is indeed a remarkable compilation, and we hope that its circulation and its usefulness may be commensurable with its conspicuous merits."—*The Schoolmaster.*

"The whole question is discussed with an elaboration, an insistence on detail, and a wisdom that mark this volume as the most important contribution to educational effort that has yet been made."
—*Contemporary Review.*

"This is a most valuable and opportune book, one to be commended to the careful attention of every serious student of the social problem."
—*The Churchman.*

"The book brims with interest to every man who recognizes the need of greater educational ideals in the masses."—*Co-operative News.*

"A work which we strongly recommend to all interested in the study of the social problem."—*The Record.*

34, Cross Street, Manchester

MANCHESTER UNIVERSITY PUBLICATIONS.
EDUCATIONAL SERIES.

" The subject of the work is one that goes to the very heart of national education, and the treatise itself lays bare with a scientific but humane hand the evils that beset our educational system, the waste of life and national energy which that system has been unable in any sufficient degree to check."—*The Spectator.*

" It is a treasure of facts and judicious opinions in the domain of the history and administration of education."—*The Athenæum.*

" The volume represents an immense service to English education, and to the future welfare and efficiency of the nation."—*Educational Times.*

No. II. THE DEMONSTRATION SCHOOL RECORD. No. I. Being Contributions to the Study of Education from the Department of Education in the University of Manchester. By Professor J. J. FINDLAY. 1s. 6d. net. (Publication No. 32, 1908.)

" This volume marks a new departure in English Educational literature . . . . Some very interesting work is being done and the most valuable part of the book is the account of the detailed methods which have been employed both in the regular teaching in the schools and in the efforts to foster the corporate interests of the children and their parents. These methods are often exceedingly suggestive, and may be studied with advantage by those who do not accept all the theories upon which they are based."—*School.*

" Professor Findlay and his skilled and experienced collaborators give an interesting account of the uses ot the demonstration classes, the nature and scope of the work done in them, and the methods adopted (as well as the underlying principles) in some of the courses of instruction."—*The Athenæum.*

" The book gives an instructive account of the attempts made to correlate the subject of school instruction, not only with each other, but also with the childrens' pursuits out of school hours. . . . The problem Professor Findlay has set himself to work out in the Demonstration School is, How far is it possible by working with the children through successive culture epochs of the human race to form within their minds not only a truer conception of human history, but also eventually a deeper comprehension of the underlying purpose and oneness of all human activities? "—*Morning Post.*

" Here the authors take us into their confidence; we are told what their view of a demonstration school is, what questions they hope to solve, and on what principles they think the answers should be sought. . . . . Those interested in educational progress will give the volume a cordial welcome."—*Nature.*

No. III. THE TEACHING OF HISTORY IN GIRLS' SCHOOLS IN NORTH AND CENTRAL GERMANY. A Report by EVA DODGE, M.A. (Publication No. 34, 1908.)

HISTORICAL SERIES.

No. I. MEDIÆVAL MANCHESTER AND THE BEGINNINGS OF LANCASHIRE. By JAMES TAIT, M.A., Professor of Ancient and Mediæval History. Demy 8vo, pp. x. 211. 7s. 6d. net. (Publication No. 3, 1904.)

" Patient and enlightened scholarship and a sense of style and proportion have enabled the writer to produce a work at once solid and readable."—*English Historical Review.*

"A welcome addition to the literature of English local history, not merely because it adds much to our knowledge of Manchester and Lancashire, but also because it displays a scientific method of treatment

MANCHESTER UNIVERSITY PUBLICATIONS.
HISTORICAL SERIES.

which is rare in this field of study in England."—Dr. Gross in *American Historical Review*.

" La collection ne pouvait débuter plus significativement et plus heureusement que par un ouvrage d'histoire du Moyen Age dû à M. Tait, car l'enseignement médiéviste est un de ceux qui font le plus d'honneur à la jeune Université de Manchester, et c'est à M. le Professeur Tait qu'il faut attribuer une bonne part de ce succès."—*Revue de Synthèse historique*.

" The two essays are models of their kind."—*Manchester Guardian*.

No. II.   INITIA OPERUM LATINORUM QUAE SAECULIS XIII., XIV., XV. ATTRIBUUNTUR. By A. G. LITTLE, M.A., Lecturer in Palæography. Demy 8vo, pp. xiii. 273 (interleaved). 15s. net.
(Publication No. 5, 1904.)

" Whoever has attempted to ascertain the contents of a Mediæval miscellany in manuscript must often have been annoyed by the occurrence of a blank space where the title of the treatise ought to be. Mr. Little has therefore earned the gratitude of all such persons by making public a collection of some 6,000 incipits, which he arranged in the first instance for his private use, in compiling a catalogue of Franciscan MSS."—*English Historical Review*.

No. III. THE OLD COLONIAL SYSTEM. By GERALD BERKELEY HERTZ, M.A., B.C.L., Lecturer in Constitutional Law. Demy 8vo, pp. xi. 232. 5s. net.   (Publication No. 7, 1905.)

" Mr. Hertz gives us an elaborate historical study of the old colonial system, which disappeared with the American Revolution. . . . . He shows a remarkable knowledge of contemporary literature, and his book may claim to be a true history of popular opinion."—*Spectator*.

" Mr. Hertz's book is one which no student of imperial developments can neglect. It is lucid, fair, thorough, and convincing."
—*Glasgow Herald*.

" Mr. Hertz's 'Old Colonial System' is based on a careful study of contemporary documents, with the result that several points of no small importance are put in a new light . . . . it is careful, honest work . . . . The story which he tells has its lesson for us."—*The Times*.

" Both the ordinary reader and the academic mind will get benefit from this well-informed and well-written book."—*Scotsman*.

" Mr. Hertz has made excellent use of contemporary literature, and has given us a very valuable and thorough critique. The book is interesting and very well written."—*American Political Science Review*.

"An interesting, valuable, and very necessary exposition of the principles underlying the colonial policy of the eighteenth century."
—*Yorkshire Post*.

" A work embodying much work and research. . . . Three most impressive chapters should be read by everyone."—*Birmingham Post*.

" Very enlightening."—*American Historical Review*.

" Timely and useful."—*Athenæum*.

No. IV. STUDIES OF ROMAN IMPERIALISM. By W. T. ARNOLD, M.A. Edited by EDWARD FIDDES, M.A., Lecturer in Ancient History, with Memoir of the Author by Mrs. HUMPHRY WARD and C. E. MONTAGUE. With a Photogravure of W. T. Arnold. Demy 8vo, 400 pp. 7s. 6d. net.
(Publication No. 16, 1906.)

" Mrs. Humphry Ward has used all her delicate and subtle art to draw a picture of her beloved brother; and his friend Mr. Montague's account of his middle life is also remarkable for its literary excellence."—*Athenæum*.

MANCHESTER UNIVERSITY PUBLICATIONS.
HISTORICAL SERIES.

"The memoir . . . . . tenderly and skilfully written by the 'sister and friend,' tells a story, which well deserved to be told, of a life rich in aspirations, interests, and friendships, and not without its measure of actual achievement."—*Tribune.*

"This geographical sense and his feeling for politics give colour to all he wrote."—*Times.*

"Anyone who desires a general account of the Empire under Augustus which is freshly and clearly written and based on wide reading will find it here."—*Manchester Guardian.*

"Nothing could be better than the sympathetic tribute which Mrs. Humphry Ward pays to her brother, or the analysis of his work and method by his colleague Mr. Montague. The two together have more stuff in them than many big books of recent biography."
—*Westminster Gazette.*

The Memoir may be had separately, price 2s. 6d. net.

No. V. CANON PIETRO CASOLA'S PILGRIMAGE TO JERUSALEM IN THE YEAR 1494. By M. M. NEWETT, B.A., formerly Jones Fellow. Demy 8vo., pp. 427. 7s. 6d. net.
(Publication No. 26, 1907.)

"Thoroughness is characteristic of introduction, the copious notes, appendix and index. . . . Miss Newett's translation is spirited and interesting . . ."—*Manchester Courier.*

"Casola's narrative richly deserved the honours of print and translation. The book is a credit to its editor and to the historical school of Manchester University."—*Morning Leader.*

"His narrative is at once simple and dignified in style, convincing and interesting in its pictures of the conditions governing travel by sea and land four centuries ago."—*Daily Telegraph.*

"The book is like a gallery of mediæval paintings, full of movement and colouring, instinct with the vitality of the time."—*Birmingham Post.*

"Miss Newett's introduction is a contribution of considerable value to the history of European commerce."—*Spectator.*

"Forms a noteworthy addition to the number of books from which a knowledge can be gained of the itineraries of the pilgrims to Palestine."
—*Scotsman.*

"The whole volume is fascinating. It presents a lively picture of bygone times, abounds in curious facts and recalls quaint and pleasing ceremonies, and exhibits the ardent pilgrim of the past in his true light. Miss Newett is alike to be congratulated on her translation, her Introduction (which takes up a third of the volume), and her notes."
—*Manchester City News.*

"The work which Miss Margaret Newett has probably saved from oblivion is as intrinsically interesting as it should prove instructive to the student of history."—*Daily News.*

"One of the most delightful narratives that record the impressions of a pious pilgrim."—*Westminster Gazette.*

"One of the most comprehensive of the itineraries is that now translated, an important feature of it being its full description of the city of Venice."—*The Times*

No. VI. HISTORICAL ESSAYS. Edited by T. F. TOUT, M.A., Professor of Mediæval and Modern History and JAMES TAIT, M.A., Professor of Ancient and Mediæval History. Demy 8vo, pp. xv. 557. 6s. net. Reissue of the Edition of 1902 with Index and New Preface
(Publication No. 27, 1907.)

"Diese zwanzig chronologisch geordneten Aufsätze heissen in der Vorrede der Herausgeber *Festchrift*, behandeln zur Hälfte ausser-englische

MANCHESTER UNIVERSITY PUBLICATIONS·
HISTORICAL SERIES.

Themata, benutzen reichlich festländische Literatur und verraten überall neben weiten Ausblicken eine methodische Schulung die der dortigen Facultät hohe Ehre macht." Professor Liebermann in *Deutsche Literaturzeitung,*
" Imperial history, local history, ecclesiastical history, economic history and the methods of historical teaching—all these are in one way or another touched upon by scholars who have collaborated in this volume. Men and women alike have devoted their time and pains to working out problems of importance and often of no slight difficulty. The result is one of which the university and city may be justly proud." The late Professor York Powell in the *Manchester Guardian.*
"Esso contiene venti lavori storici dettati, quattro da professori e sedici da licenziati del Collegio, e sono tutto scritti appositamente e condotti secondo le più rigorose norme della critica e su documenti." R. Predelli in *Nuovo Archivio Veneto.*
"La variété des sujets et l'érudition avec laquelle ils sont traités font grand honneur à la manière dont l'histoire est enseigné à Owens College." *Revue Historique.*
"No one who reads these essays will do so without acknowledging their ability, both in originality and research. They deal with historic subjects from the beginnings of Cæsar-worship to the detention of Napoleon at St. Helena, and they deal with them in a thoroughgoing fashion." *Guardian.*
"Par nature, c'est un recueil savant, qui témoigne du respect et de l'émulation que sait exercer pour les études historiques la jeune et déjà célèbre université." *Revue d'histoire ecclésiastique* (Louvain).
" All these essays reach a high level ; they avoid the besetting sin of most of our present historical writing, which consists of serving up a hash of what other historians have written flavoured with an original spice of error. . . . . They are all based on original research and written by specialists." Professor A. F. Pollard in the *English Historical Review.*
"Sie bilden einen schönen Beweis fur die rationelle Art, mit der dort dieses Studium betrieben wird." Professor O. Weber in *Historische Zeitschrift.*
The Index can be purchased separately price 6d.

MEDICAL SERIES.

No. I. SKETCHES OF THE LIVES AND WORK OF THE HONORARY MEDICAL STAFF OF THE ROYAL INFIRMARY. From its foundation in 1752 to 1830, when it became the Royal Infirmary. By EDWARD MANSFIELD BROCKBANK, M.D., M.R.C.P. Crown 4to. (illustrated). Pp. vii. 311. 15s. net.
(Publication No. 1, 1904.)
" Dr. Brockbank's is a book of varied interest. It also deserves a welcome as one of the earliest of the ' Publications of the University of Manchester.' "—*Manchester Guardian.*
" We have a valuable contribution to local Medical Literature."
—*Daily Dispatch.*

No. II. PRACTICAL PRESCRIBING AND DISPENSING. For Medical Students. By WILLIAM KIRKBY, sometime Lecturer in Pharmacognosy in the Owens College, Manchester. Crown 8vo, 220 pp. 5s. net.
(Publication No. 2, 1904, Second edition, 1906.)
" The whole of the matter bears the impress of that technical skill and thoroughness with which Mr. Kirkby's name must invariably be

MANCHESTER UNIVERSITY PUBLICATIONS.
MEDICAL SERIES.

associated, and the book must be welcomed as one of the most useful recent additions to the working library of prescribers and dispensers."
—*Pharmaceutical Journal.*

"Thoroughly practical text-books on the subject are so rare, that we welcome with pleasure Mr. William Kirkby's 'Practical Prescribing and Dispensing.' The book is written by a pharmacist expressly for medical students, and the author has been most happy in conceiving its scope and arrangement."—*British Medical Journal.*

"The work appears to be peculiarly free from blemishes and particularly full in practical detail. It is manifestly the work of one who is a skilled chemist, and an expert pharmacist, and who knows not only the requirements of the modern student but the best way in which his needs may be met."—*Medical Press.*

"This is a very sensible and useful manual."—*The Hospital.*

"The book will be found very useful to any students during a course of practical dispensing."—*St. Bartholomew's Hospital Journal.*

"The book is a model, being tutorial from beginning to end."
—*The Chemist and Druggist.*

No. III. HANDBOOK OF SURGICAL ANATOMY. By G. A. WRIGHT, B.A., M.B. (Oxon.), F.R.C.S., Professor of Systematic Surgery, and C. H. PRESTON, M.D., F.R.C.S., L.D.S., Lecturer on Dental Anatomy; Assistant Dental Surgeon to the Victoria Dental Hospital of Manchester. Crown 8vo, pp. ix. 205. Second edition. 5s. net.   (Publication No. 6, 1905.)

"We can heartily recommend the volume to students, and especially to those preparing for a final examination in surgery."—*Hospital.*

"Dr. Wright and Dr. Preston have produced a concise and very readable little handbook of surgical applied anatomy. . . . The subject matter of the book is well arranged and the marginal notes in bold type facilitate reference to any desired point."—*Lancet.*

No. IV. A COURSE OF INSTRUCTION IN OPERATIVE SURGERY in the University of Manchester. By WILLIAM THORBURN, M.D., B.S. (Lond.), F.R.C.S., Lecturer in Operative Surgery. Crown 8vo, pp. 75. 2s. 6d. net.
                                      (Publication No. 11, 1906.)

"This little book gives the junior student all that he wants, and nothing that he does not want. Its size is handy, and altogether for its purpose it is excellent."—*University Review.*

"As a working guide it is excellent."—*Edinburgh Medical Journal.*

No. V. A HANDBOOK OF LEGAL MEDICINE. By W. SELLARS, M.D. (London), of the Middle Temple and Northern Circuit, Barrister-at-law. With Illustrations. Crown 8vo, pp. vii. 233. 7s. 6d. net.   (Publication No. 14, 1906.)

"This is quite one of the best books of the kind we have come across."—*Law Times.*

No. VI. A CATALOGUE OF THE PATHOLOGICAL MUSEUM OF THE UNIVERSITY OF MANCHESTER. Edited by J. LORRAIN SMITH, M.A., M.D. (Edin.), Professor of Pathology. Crown 4to, 1260 pp. 7s. 6d. net.   (Publication No. 15, 1906.)

"The catalogue compares very favourably with others of a similar character, and, apart from its value for teaching purposes in an important medical school such as that of the University of Manchester, it is capable of being of great assistance to others as a work of reference."
—*Edinburgh Medical Journal.*

SHERRATT & HUGHES

MANCHESTER UNIVERSITY PUBLICATIONS·
MEDICAL SERIES.

"In conclusion we need only say that Professor Lorrain Smith has performed the most essential part of his task—the description of the specimens—excellently, and an honourable mention must be made of the book as a publication."—*British Medical Journal.*

No. VII. HANDBOOK OF DISEASES OF THE HEART. By GRAHAM STEELL, M.D., F.R.C.P., Professor of Medicine, and Physician to the Manchester Royal Infirmary. Crown 8vo, pp. xii. 389, 11 plates (5 in colours), and 100 illustrations in the text. 7s. 6d. net. (Publication No. 20, 1906.)

"It more truly reflects modern ideas of heart disease than any book we are acquainted with, and therefore may be heartily recommended to our readers."—*Treatment.*

"We regard this volume as an extremely useful guide to the study of diseases of the heart, and consider that no better introduction to the subject could possibly have been written."—*Medical Times and Hospital Gazette.*

"We can cordially recommend Dr. Steell's book as giving an excellent and thoroughly practical account of the subject of which it treats."—*Edinburgh Medical Review.*

No. VIII. JULIUS DRESCHFELD. IN MEMORIAM. Medical Studies by his colleagues and pupils at the Manchester University and the Royal Infirmary. (Publication No. 35, 1908.)

PHYSICAL SERIES.

No. I. THE PHYSICAL LABORATORIES OF THE UNIVER-SITY OF MANCHESTER. A record of 25 years' work. Demy 8vo, pp. 142, 10 Plates, 4 Plans. 5s. net. (Publication No. 13, 1906.)

This volume contains an illustrated description of the Physical, Electrical Engineering, and Electro-Chemistry Laboratories of the Manchester University, also a complete Biographical and Bibliographical Record of those who have worked in the Physics Department of the University during the past 25 years.

"The book is excellently got up, and contains a description of the department of physics and its equipment, a short biographical sketch of the Professor with a list of his scientific writings and a well-executed portrait and a record of the career of students and others who have passed through Dr. Schuster's hands. Alumni of Owens will welcome the volume as an interesting link with their alma mater."—*Glasgow Herald.*

"This interesting and valuable contribution to the history of the Manchester University also contains several illustrations, and forms the first of the 'physical series' of the publications of the University of Manchester."—*The Times*

"A record of achievement of which no man need be ashamed"—*Westminster Gazette.*

"It is a memorial of which any man would be justly proud, and the University of which he is both an alumnus and a professor may well share that pride."—*Manchester Gaurdian.*

PUBLIC HEALTH SERIES.

No. I. ARCHIVES OF THE PUBLIC HEALTH LABORATORY OF THE UNIVERSITY OF MANCHESTER. Edited by A. SHERIDAN DELÉPINE, M.Sc., M.B., Ch.M., Director of the Laboratory and Procter Professor of Comparative Pathology and Bacteriology. Crown 4to. pp. iv. 451. £1. 1s. net. (Publication No. 12, 1906.)

34, Cross Street, Manchester

MANCHESTER UNIVERSITY PUBLICATIONS.
PUBLIC HEALTH SERIES.

"The University of Manchester has taken the important and highly commendable step of commencing the publication of the archives of its Public Health Laboratory, and has issued, under the able and judicious editorship of Professor Sheridan Delépine, the first volume of a series that promises to be of no small interest and value alike to members of the medical profession and to those of the laity. . . . Original communications bearing upon diseases which are prevalent in the districts surrounding Manchester, or dealing with food- and water-supplies, air, disposal of refuse, sterilisation and disinfection and kindred subjects, will be published in future volumes; and it is manifest that these, as they successively appear, will form a constantly increasing body of trustworthy information upon subjects which are not only of the highest interest to the profession but of supreme importance to the public."—
The Lancet.

"It is safe to say that as these volumes accumulate they will form one of the most important works of reference on questions of public health, and ought, at all events, to be in the library of every public authority."—*Manchester Guardian.*

"The volume . . . . speaks well for the activity of investigation in Manchester."—*Lancet.*

THEOLOGICAL SERIES.

No. I. INAUGURAL LECTURES delivered during the Session 1904–5, by the Professors and Lecturers of the Faculty of Theology, viz. :—

Prof. T. F. Tout, M.A.; Prof. A. S. Peake, B.D.; Prof. H. W. Hogg, M.A.; Prof. T. W. Rhys Davids, LL.D.; Rev. W. F. Adeney, D.D.; Rev. A. Gordon, M.A.; Rev. L. Hassé, B.D.; Rev. Canon E. L. HICKS, M.A.; Rev. H. D. Lockett, M.A.; Rev. R. Mackintosh, D.D.; Rev. J. T. Marshall, D.D.; Rev. J. H. Moulton, D.Litt.

Edited by A. S. PEAKE, B.D., Dean of the Faculty.
Demy 8vo, pp. xi. 296. 7s. 6d. net.

(Publication No. 9, 1905.)

"The lectures, while scholarly, are at the same time popular, and will be found interesting and instructive by those who are not theologians. . . . The entire series is excellent, and the volume deserves a wide circulation."—*Scotsman.*

"This is a very welcome volume . . . All these lectures were delivered to popular audiences, yet they are far from superficial, and will be found of great value to busy pastors and teachers."—*Christian World.*

"We welcome the volume as a most auspicious sign of the times."
—*Spectator.*

"The lectures themselves give a valuable conspectus of the present position of Theological research. . . . They are, of course, not addressed to experts, but they are exceedingly valuable, even when allowance is made for their more or less popular form."—*Examiner.*

"The whole volume forms a very important and valuable contribution to the cause of Theological learning."—*Record.*

"This is a most interesting and valuable book, the appearance of which at the present moment is singularly significant. . . . But it is impossible in a brief review to indicate all the treasures of this rich volume, to read which carefully is to be introduced to the varied wealth of modern Biblical scholarship."—*Baptist.*

"This volume is of the most exceptional value and interest."
—*Expository Times.*

60, Chandos Street, London, W.C.

SHERRATT & HUGHES

MANCHESTER UNIVERSITY PUBLICATIONS.
THEOLOGICAL SERIES.

"This is a book of more than common interest."
—*Review of Theology and Philosophy.*
"The writers of these lectures do not attempt to offer more than samples of their wares : but what is given is good, and it may be seen that theology without tests is destitute neither of scientific value nor of human interests."—*Athenæum.*

LECTURES.

No. I. GARDEN CITIES (Warburton Lecture). By RALPH NEVILLE, K.C. 6d. net. (Lecture No. 1, 1905.)

No. II. THE BANK OF ENGLAND AND THE STATE (A Lecture). By Sir FELIX SCHUSTER. 6d. net. (Lecture No. 2, 1905.)

No. III. BEARING AND IMPORTANCE OF COMMERCIAL TREATIES IN THE TWENTIETH CENTURY. By Sir THOMAS BARCLAY. 6d. net. (Lecture No. 3, 1906.)

No. IV. THE SCIENCE OF LANGUAGE AND THE STUDY OF THE GREEK TESTAMENT (A Lecture). By JAMES HOPE MOULTON, M.A., Litt.D. 6d. net. (Lecture No. 4, 1906.)

No. V. THE GENERAL MEDICAL COUNCIL: ITS POWERS AND ITS WORK (A Lecture). By DONALD MACALISTER, M.A., M.D., B.Sc., D.C.L., LL.D. 6d. net.
(Lecture No. 5, 1906.)

No. VI. THE CONTRASTS IN DANTE (A Lecture). By the Hon. WILLIAM WARREN VERNON, M.A. 6d. net.
(Lecture No. 6, 1906.)

No. VII. THE PRESERVATION OF PLACES OF INTEREST OR BEAUTY (A Lecture). By Sir ROBERT HUNTER. 6d. net.
(Lecture No. 7, 1907.)

CALENDARS.

CALENDAR OF THE VICTORIA UNIVERSITY OF MAN-CHESTER. Session 1904-5. Demy 8vo, 1100 pp. 3s. net.
(Publication No. 17.)

CALENDAR OF THE VICTORIA UNIVERSITY OF MAN-CHESTER. Session 1905-6. Demy 8vo, 1200 pp. 3s. net.
(Publication No. 18.)

CALENDAR OF THE VICTORIA UNIVERSITY OF MAN-CHESTER. Session 1906-7. Demy 8vo, 1300 pp. 3s. net.
(Publication No. 19.)

CALENDAR OF THE VICTORIA UNIVERSITY OF MAN-CHESTER. Session 1907-8. Demy 8vo, 1400 pp. 3s. net.
(Publication No. 28.)

CALENDAR OF THE VICTORIA UNIVERSITY OF MAN-CHESTER. Session 1908-9. Demy 8vo, 1460 pp. 3s. net.
(Publication No. 37.)

THE REGISTER OF GRADUATES OF THE UNIVERSITY OF MANCHESTER UP TO JULY 1908.

60, Chandos Street, London, W.C.

MANCHESTER UNIVERSITY PUBLICATIONS.

The following are in preparation and will be issued shortly :—

Celtic Series. No. I.

AN INTRODUCTION TO EARLY WELSH, By the late Prof.
J. STRACHAN, M.A., LL.D. Edited and completed by Prof. KUNO
MEYER, Ph.D. Demy 8vo.

This work will comprise a Grammar of Early Welsh with special
reference to Middle-Welsh prose. To the grammar will be added
selected passages from Early Welsh texts in prose and verse, together
with notes and a glossary compiled by TIMOTHY LEWIS, B.A.
[In October.

A GLOSSARY TO THE BLACK BOOK OF CHIRK MANU-
SCRIPT OF THE WELSH LAWS. By TIMOTHY LEWIS, B.A.
Demy 8vo.

This will include a complete glossary to the oldest copy of the " Laws
of Howel Dda," contained in the " Black Book of Chirk," and will be
based on the photographic facsimile of that manuscript which is about to
be published by Dr. J. Gwenogvryn Evans in his collection of Welsh
texts. [In Preparation.

THE LANGUAGE OF THE ANNALS OF ULSTER. By TOMAS
O'MÁILLE, M.A. Demy 8vo.

The objects of this dissertation are firstly to investigate the date at
which certain old-Irish phonological developments took place, and
secondly to give an account of old-Irish declension as evidenced by the
language of the Annals of Ulster. An Appendix on the analysis of
Irish personal names is appended. [In Preparation.

Economic Series.

SOME ELECTRO-CHEMICAL CENTRES. Gartside Report. By
J. N. PRING, M.Sc. [In the Press.

Historical Series.

STUDIES SUPPLEMENTARY TO STUBBS' CONSTITUTIONAL
HISTORY. Vol I. By CH. PETIT-DUTAILIS, Lit.D., rector of
the University of Grenoble. Translated from the French by W. E.
RHODES, M.A., and edited by Prof. JAMES TAIT, M.A.

This work will consist of the translation of the studies and notes
appended by Prof. Petit-Dutaillis to his translation into French of the
first volume of Stubbs' Constitutional History of England. It is believed
that they will present to English students and teachers a summary of
the results of recent historical research so far as they throw light upon
or modify the conclusions expressed thirty years ago by the late Bishop
Stubbs. [In October.

HANES GRUFFYDD AP CYNAN. The Welsh text with translation,
introduction, and notes by ARTHUR JONES, M.A., Jones Fellow in
History. Demy 8vo. [In Preparation.

60, Chandos Street, London, W.C.

SHERRATT & HUGHES

MANCHESTER UNIVERSITY PUBLICATIONS.

THE CROMWELLIAN CONQUEST AND SETTLEMENT OF IRELAND. By ROBERT DUNLOP, M.A., formerly Berkeley Fellow. Demy 8vo.

This work will consist of a series of unpublished documents relating to the History of Ireland from 1651 to 1659, arranged, modernized, and edited, with introduction, notes, etc., by Mr. DUNLOP.

[*In Preparation.*

Medical Series.

HANDBOOK OF INFECTIOUS DISEASES. By R. W. MARSDEN, M.D. [*Immediately.*

MODERN PROBLEMS IN PSYCHIATRY. By E. LUGARO, Professor of Nervous and Mental Diseases in the University of Modena. Translated from the Italian by DAVID ORR, M.D., Assistant Medical Officer and Pathologist to the County Asylum, Prestwich; and R. G. Rows, M.D., Assistant Medical Officer and Pathologist to the County Asylum, Lancaster. With an introduction by T. S. CLOUSTON, M.D., Physician Superintendent, Royal Asylum, Morningside, and Lecturer on Mental Diseases in Edinburgh University.

Deals with the problems met with in studying the causation of insanity. These problems are discussed under the headings of psychological, anatomical, pathogenetic, etiological, nosological, social and practical. There are 13 illustrations in the anatomical section.

[*In Preparation.*

DISEASES OF THE EAR. By W. MILLIGAN, M.D., Lecturer on Diseases of the Ear and Nasal Surgeon to the Manchester Royal Infirmary. [*In Preparation.*

DISEASES OF THE EYE. By C. E. GLASCOTT, M.D., Lecturer on Ophthalmology, and A. HILL GRIFFITH, M.D., Ophthalmic Surgeon to the Manchester Royal Infirmary. [*In Preparation.*

HANDBOOK OF NERVOUS DISEASES. By JUDSON S. BURY, M.D., Lecturer on Clinical Neurology and Physician to the Manchester Royal Infirmary. [*In Preparation.*

Zoological Series.

STRUCTURE, DEVELOPMENT AND BIONOMICS OF THE HOUSE FLY. By C. GORDON HEWITT, M.Sc. [*In Preparation.*

The following works, though not technically Publications of the University of Manchester, are also issued from the University Press :—

MELANDRA CASTLE, being the Report of the Manchester and District Branch of the Classical Association for 1905. Edited by R. S. CONWAY, Litt.D. Introduction by Rev. E. L. HICKS, M.A. Demy 8vo. Illustrated. 5s. net.

TRANSACTIONS OF THE INTERNATIONAL UNION FOR CO-OPERATION IN SOLAR RESEARCH (Vol. i., First and Second Conferences). Demy 8vo, 260 pp. and plate. 7s. 6d. net.

THE BOOK OF RUTH (Unpointed Text). 6d. net.

THE BOOK OF AMOS. (Unpointed Text.) 6d. net.

60, Chandos Street, London, W.C.

MANCHESTER UNIVERSITY PUBLICATIONS.

SCENES FROM THE RUDENS OF PLAUTUS, with a Translation
into English Verse. Edited by R. S. Conway, Litt.D., Professor of
Latin in the University. 6d. net.

THE MOSTELLARIA OF PLAUTUS. Acting edition with a translation into English Verse. Edited by G. Norwood, M.A. 1s. net.

THE TEACHING OF HISTORY AND OTHER PAPERS. By H.
L. Withers. Edited by J. H. Fowler. Crown 8vo, 270 pp.
4s. 6d. net.

"An interesting memorial of a teacher who was a real enthusiast for
education."—*The Times*.

"We can cordially commend this little book to the somewhat limited
but slowly widening circle who are likely to be interested in educational
principles and organization."—*The Guardian*.

A TARDINESS IN NATURE AND OTHER PAPERS. By Mary
Christie. Edited, with Introductory Note and Memoir, by Maud
Withers. Crown 8vo, 331 pp. 3s. net.

"The essays upon Thackeray, George Eliot, and R. L. Stevenson in
this volume could scarcely be bettered."—*The Guardian*.

"The life-story of a quite remarkable woman—of a woman who used
her gifts always to the furthering of all that is sweetest and noblest in
life."—*Tribune*.

MUSICAL CRITICISMS. By Arthur Johnstone. With a Memoir
of the Author by Henry Reece and Oliver Elton. Crown 8vo,
225 pp. 5s. net.

"Without the smallest affectation or laboured attempts at smartness,
Mr. Johnstone contrived always to throw fresh light on the matter in
hand, and at the same time to present his opinions in a form which
could be understood and enjoyed by the non-musical reader."—
Westminster Gazette.

"Everyone who welcomes guidance as to what is best in music,
everyone who watches with some degree of fascination the power of
analysis, everyone who reads with a sense of satisfaction English, as it
may be written by a master of the craft, should read this book."—
The Musical World.

MANCHESTER BOYS. By C. E. B. Russell. With an Introduction by E. T. Campagnac. Crown 8vo. 2s. 6d. net.

"Mr. Charles E. B. Russell has written a most interesting and
thought-compelling book on a subject of almost vital importance."—
Yorkshire Post.

"Altogether it is an inspiring book."—*Liverpool Daily Post and
Mercury*.

60, Chandos Street, London, W.C.